HOMOSEXUALITY IN THE CHURCH

A SECOND LOOK AT THE "RE-IMAGINING" CONFERENCES

JUDY MCKENZIE MCCLARY

WILL THE REAL CHURCH PLEASE STAND UP SERIES

Magnolia Publications

Homosexuality in the Church – A Second Look at the "REimagining" Conferences by Judy McKenzie McClary
Published by Magnolia Publications

This book or parts thereof may not be reproduced in any form, stored in a retrieval system, or transmitted in any form by any means—electronic, mechanical, photocopy, recording, or otherwise—without prior written permission of the publisher, except as provided by United States of America copyright law.

Unless otherwise noted, all Scripture quotations are from the New King James Version of the Bible. Copyright © 1979, 1980, 1982 by Thomas Nelson, Inc., publishers. Used by permission.

Scripture quotations marked AMP are from the Amplified Bible. Old Testament copyright © 1965, 1987 by the Zondervan Corporation. The Amplified New Testament copyright © 1954, 1958, 1987 by the Lockman Foundation. Used by permission.

Scripture quotations marked NIV are from the Holy Bible, New International Version of the Bible. Copyright © 1973, 1978, 1984, International Bible Society. Used by permission.

Scripture quotations marked NLT are taken from the Holy Bible, New Living Translation, copyright © 1996, 2004, 2007 by Tyndale House Foundation. Used by permission of Tyndale House Publishers, Inc., Carol Stream, Illinois 60188. All rights reserved.

Copyright © 2015 by Judy McKenzie McClary
All rights reserved

International Standard Book Number: 978-0-9747292-3-7

Printed in the United States of America
Available from Amazon.com and other retail outlets

This book is lovingly dedicated to my husband, Charles, who has consistently given me support and encouragement as I researched and wrote on the essential issue of baptism and the Church.

CONTENTS

Foreword 1

PART I
GODDESSES IN THE CHURCH

1 Two Simple Questions 5
2 Tugging at Loose Ends... 9
3 A Bowling Trip 15
4 RE-imagining the Church.. 21
5 Recycling Sophia 31
6 Chicken or the Egg?.. 37
7 A Path to the Pulpit 43
8 Is the Church at Risk? 47
9 Checking the Fruit 51
10 Delayed Justice 57
11 Page from an Ancient Playbook............................... 61
12 A Secret & Terrible Conspiracy............................... 65

PART II
THE MISSING FACTOR

13 Time Warp 85
14 Sun Worship – The Smoking Gun 93
15 Sun Worship & the Catholic Church........................ 101
13 Christmas, Easter & *what?* 109
13 The Missing Puzzle Piece 117
13 Two Trees 121

Appendix i Ten Myths about Infant Baptism... 127
Appendix ii Back to Faith Alone 137
Author's Page.. 143
Books by Author 145
Bibliography.. 147

FOREWARD

Five hundred years after the Great Reformation has come and gone, the Lutheran denomination (ELCA), the Presbyterian church (USA), the Episcopal church and United Methodist churches sponsored a "RE-imagining" conference where a goddess was worshiped, the blood of Jesus ridiculed, and the born-again experience denied.

The Bible says a good tree *cannot* produce bad fruit and a bad tree *cannot* produce good fruit. Yet as early as 1991, many churches under the umbrella of the ELCA were considering leaving because of pagan practices advocated by their leadership.

At that time, a stand was taken against time-honored biblical mores even though it was billed as 'just running it up the old flagpole,' as they say in advertising circles, to see whether it would fly. Their attitude seemed to be, if it won't fly today, maybe it will fly tomorrow.

This began a desensitization process, a gradual tearing down of the belief system of staunch Lutherans, a breach in literal values as taught in the Bible. The draft intentionally forced open doors of thought that eventually would lead to an increased acceptance of anti-God, anti-biblical sexual practices. The possibility of ordaining clergy engaged in *practicing* homosexual relationships was never cracked open.

Questions were raised at that time as to the belief system of a mainline denominational church that would open such doors. Some wondered if there could be something *in the roots* of the Lutheran church going back to the time of its inception that caused it to bring forth such bad fruit? And there were questions about Martin Luther's part. Wasn't he the great hero of the Christian church—one of the true great Church fathers?

A lowly-but-nagging voice asks, what if—just what if—Luther was not as the Christian church has portrayed him for the past five hundred years? Would people begin to search for Bible truth themselves as Luther did so many years ago when he discovered *his* church had failed *him*? Or would they just throw up their hands and turn away from God altogether? That is a very real danger, you know.

One thing the churches that sponsored the "REimagining" conferences held in common is their mutual practice of infant baptism, information that will become very important in unraveling the mystery of where these aberrant beliefs originated.

But can this alone account for the bad fruit the infant baptism denominations are bearing? And what in our roots has precipitated this great falling away?

And, last but not least, how do we find our way back?

PART I

GODDESSES IN THE CHURCH

1
TWO SIMPLE QUESTIONS

In the fall of 1991, I had two questions on my mind. My first question was why I couldn't find any mention of infant baptism in the Bible. My second concern was whether we should remain affiliated with the ELCA (Evangelical Lutheran Church in America)?

The first question had come about while I was preparing Bible curriculum for our 5,000-member ELCA Lutheran church. I needed answers to why I couldn't find infant baptism in the Bible? Our church taught a baptism of babies and that 'baptism saves.' It even listed 'baptism saves' as the salvation doctrine that Martin Luther put in the *Augsburg Confession* without mentioned the blood of Christ even once although Luther was famous for faith *'alone.'*

The second question wasn't so immediate for me. If our church remained affiliated with the ELCA did not affect me as personally. Church leaders had asked members to fast and pray over the matter because the issue of staying or leaving the ELCA had accelerated due to a *draft on human sexuality* currently being circulated by ELCA leadership in which they appeared to champion the homosexual lifestyle.

Still, as mentioned earlier, the infant baptism

question was the most pressing to me. Along with countless other churches, our church taught a different water baptism than the one found in the Bible. I was determined to prove that our baptism of infants was the right one. After all, no greater personage than Martin Luther had taught that we were literally 'saved'[1] in the waters of baptism and going to heaven because our parents had baptized us as infants.

However, I was unsuccessful in my search. Using the *Strong's Concordance of Bible Words* (which is an unusual concordance in that it lists each word in the Bible in both English and Greek, its meaning and then shows the verses in which it occurs), I was still unable to find anything to verify infant baptism.

Finally I had made a phone call to our senior pastor to ask for his help. During our conversation, he referred to infant baptism as 'a thinly-veiled' *form of circumcision.* That was a new term to me; I hadn't heard it before and had no way of knowing that such a simple-sounding phrase was about to put me on a path of discovery that would take years to unravel.

My search would lead me through the Reformation and back even earlier to the alliance made between the church of Rome and the Roman government. It was there that I would discover a schism brought about by infant baptism which caused various groups who refused to practice it and considered it heresy to be burned at the stake and/or drowned.

I wondered why this had not been discussed from the pulpit? And who was right? I came across a decree issued as early as 413 A.D. by the Roman Catholic church that stated that any Anabaptist (rebaptizer) was to be put to death.[2] This surprised me because in checking Scripture I turned up only one water baptism and that was the one given by St. Peter on the Day of Pentecost when the Church commenced.[3]

My search would eventually lead me to the unintended acquisition of a thorough working knowledge of the ancient mystery religions in my search to find the origins of infant baptism.

It wasn't a pretty story.

---

[1] The word "saved" is somewhat of a misnomer but because evangelical Christians use it indiscriminately while meaning "justified," this book also uses the vernacular of the day. Western Christians use the term "saved" when they talk about that moment in time when they receive a converted heart but this is inaccurate because the Bible uses the term "justified" in referring to that moment. It reserves the term "saved" for the making-us-whole that occurs *after we are justified.* In other words, "saved" refers to what God does AFTER we are born again; i.e., the deliverance, healing and restoration that begins to take place in every area of our lives after our conversion. "Saved" means being made whole AFTER our conversion experience. Justified—*just-as-if-I'd-never-sinned*—means the righteousness imparted to us when we first put our faith in the finished work of the cross. Thus when reading the Bible, it is important to pay attention to whether "saved" or "justified" is used in a verse in order to extract the correct biblical meaning.

[2] van Braght (the Bloody Edict by emperors Theodosius and Honorius), 198.

[3] Acts 2:38

2

TUGGING AT LOOSE ENDS

It was the spring of 1992. I was completely unaware that elsewhere in the country the seeds of the RE-imagining conferences were already germinating. I was completing my first year at a two-year Lutheran Bible school (for laypeople), and had learned a great many things during that time—many of which were not part of the coursework.

One of those things was that we are not joined to the Body of Christ through infant baptism. Another was that we are in imminent danger of being disqualified for eternal life if we elevate infant baptism to a position of being equal or above Christ's finished work of the Cross. Another was that Martin Luther *didn't really believe* salvation was by faith alone—at least that was not what was put into the *Augsburg Confession*. As revolutionary as these realizations were to me at the time—it was just the beginning.

I wrote the first letter to our church after I realized that Luther had allowed his Reformation-starting revelation for which he is still famous—"saved by faith alone"—to be lost sometime between when he was declared a heretic whose life was in danger[1] and when he left his life-preserving, hiding-place at

Wartburg castle to return unannounced to his hometown of Wittenberg, Germany.[2]

For the first time, Luther would publicly embrace infant baptism *as necessary for salvation*—and effectively leave behind his revelation of salvation by faith alone in the finished work of the cross.[3] The truth of this doctrine had revolutionized those to whom he brought biblical evidence—both his students at Wittenberg University and his parishioners at Wittenberg Church.

When Luther was excommunicated at the Diet of Worms and went into hiding in the Wartburg castle at the urging of his benefactor, the Elecktor Frederick, he was safe from the violence of men. His writings from that time, however, show he encountered unexpected spiritual and physical trials as he sat alone day after day in the abandoned castle.[4] Ten months later, when his friend, Philip Melanchthon cried out for help to regain control over the swelling tide of reformation, Luther left the safety of the castle and returned to public life.

Melanchthon, Luther's longtime associate, had panicked because three men were preaching in the streets of Wittenberg and saying that his reformation had not gone far enough. In his new Lutheran church, Luther would remove many false beliefs but he would leave in infant baptism. Now they had discovered—just as I had—that infant baptism could not be found in the Bible. They also insisted that the Holy Spirit was for today's church as well as the early Church. Now that copies of Scripture in the national language were pouring out of the new Guttenberg presses; people were hungrily reading them and finding the truth for themselves.

Other reform leaders were rising up, too, and they headed directly to the most important issue of all: "What must *I do* to be saved?[5] These men were not finding infant baptism to be the answer, any more than I had for the Bible sets forth definite standards for the way of salvation.

> ... Repent, and let every one of you be baptized in the name of Jesus Christ for the remission of sins; and you shall receive the gift of the Holy Spirit.
>
> —Acts 2:38

Bypassing the Church of Rome entirely, these new leaders were studying the teachings of Jesus Christ, and of John the Baptist, and all the prophets before him. What they found, read: "Repent, for the kingdom of heaven is at hand."[6] But their discovery did not stop there. They found that the next step after repentance—that of immersion baptism—could not be reasoned away by clever sleight of hand:[7]

Thus it was that 'the infant baptism question' emerged just months into what would become known as the great Reformation. With it came the rising tide of disagreement over infant baptism. It was this that prompted Philip Melanchthon's terrified call to Luther, begging him to come out of hiding.

When studying at the Bible School connected with our Lutheran church, I questioned my teachers, pastors and finally the president of our school in my attempt to validate infant baptism. Finally, my questions elicited the reluctant response from the founder that infant baptism had once bothered him, too. He then shared the information that when he was graduated from a Lutheran seminary, they would not ordain him because he was married to a Mennonite woman. He said it was because the Mennonites had some trouble over infant baptism with the Lutherans and Catholics.

At the time, it was hard for me to believe that they would be prejudiced against such a godly woman as his wife. Later in my search for the truth I discovered the reason—it was the guilty consciences of the Lutherans and the Catholics over the history of how their churches had murdered the Mennonites because they would not practice infant baptism.

So, in my research begun so enthusiastically, I now pulled back. I did not want to go down this path. When I had begun what I thought was a simple journey, I naively thought it would end by showcasing Martin Luther's triumph in starting the great Reformation and bringing the church out of darkness. I had only wanted to understand his reasoning for choosing a baptism of infants over the full-immersion, after-conversion water baptism that was being taught in some of our neighboring churches.

I had not intended to get sidetracked into the centuries-old mystery of how it happened that the Christian church had divided over water baptism. Yet, my discovery turned out to be just the first of many such 'loose strings' that, no matter which end I pulled, infant baptism would be at the center.

[1] 'To "ban" someone's life is a procedure whereby the Roman Catholic church does not immediately execute a person but rather takes away their legal right to live. If the man (or woman) has enemies, this allowed the Catholic church to keep their hands clean while giving the man's enemies the opportunity to take that person's life without fear of legal recrimination.

[2] Theologians have long known about this change, even using the phrases "young Luther" and "old Luther" to differentiate between the early teachings and the later teachings of Luther.

[3] Though Luther continued to use the phrase "salvation is by faith alone," he now limited its meaning to a criticism of pardons and indulgences (supposed forgiveness of past sins and future sins, respectively, in exchange for money or valuables) and the adoration and image-making of saints within the Roman church.

[4] These difficulties have already been written about at length in many well-written books. A search of the internet or most public libraries will produce numerous titles for those who want to know more.

[5] Acts 16:30

[6] "From that time, Jesus began to preach and to say, "Repent, for the kingdom of heaven is at hand."" Matthew 4:17

[7] Mark 16:16

3

A BOWLING TRIP

I had started out with two simple questions--is infant baptism found in the Bible? And should our ELCA Lutheran church be concerned about the direction their leadership was taking?

I knew the lack of Bible verses to authenticate infant baptism was very serious in our church because Sunday after Sunday infant baptism ceremonies were performed and it was impressed upon the congregation that 'baptism saves' yet there was no Scripture in the Bible to validate it.

A further concern was that its entry into the Church had divided the Church into two camps. As I researched further, I discovered that it was Martin Luther's closest friend and longtime associate, Philip Melanchthon, who was responsible for bringing in the belief that baptism saves, instead of Luther's God-given revelation that one is saved by faith.

It was Melanchthon who inserted the words "saved by baptism" into the *Augsburg Confession,* thus negating Luther's well known position that salvation is by *faith alone.* He was able to do this because he alone attended a meeting with the Roman Catholic church and presented a position paper called the *Augsburg Confession*. To make reconciliation more likely, Melanchthon had added in 'baptism saves' and removed all mention of the blood of Christ. When Luther finally heard that his revelation had not been included in the Augsburg Confession, he protested feebly and then moved on. Thus it was that infant baptism ('baptism saves') entered the Lutheran statement of faith.

Therefore, it was Melanchthon—and not Luther!—that blotted out the revelation that we are saved by faith alone. And, indeed, it is Melanchthon who is considered in contemporary seminaries to be the Lutheran theologian—*not Luther!*

While Luther was still sequestered away in the abandoned Wartburg castle, Melanchthon had begged him to come out of hiding to settle some matters that were being exposed on the streets of Luther's hometown of Wittenberg. It was over the matter of whether or not infant baptism was a legitimate doctrine of Christianity.

Melanchthon knew Luther was the one man with the clout to settle the infant baptism question. There were men preaching in the streets of Wittenberg that the Reformation had not gone far enough—that infant baptism should be removed from church doctrines. They claimed it, too, was only a tradition of the Catholic church and must be removed.[1]

Melanchthon was against removing it. However, because of all that followed, it seems likely that it may have been the belief "*baptism saves*" for which Melanchthon was concerned and did not want that belief to fall into obscurity. For contrary to some reports, Melanchthon and Luther did not always see eye-to-eye. It was Melanchthon who harbored a secret wish to be back in the good graces of the Roman church which was all-powerful in that day because of its alliance with the Roman government. They provided the legal teeth for the enforcement of any church decrees (a holdover from the days of Roman emperors ruling as gods—thus being both head of religion and head of state). Melanchthon liked that.

Luther often chided Melanchthon for being such a devoted follower of astrology and the zodiac, quite curious pastimes for someone choosing the salvation doctrine of a Christian church.[2] I might have chosen to overlook Melanchthon's devotion to astrology like Luther did because I hated the idea of getting too familiar with astrology, let alone the full-blown occult.

I contemplated simply dropping the whole tangled mess—and I would have if it hadn't been for a bowling stint my eldest daughter felt she just had to take right when I was getting to this point in my research—that changed everything.

As it happened, early one morning my daughter asked me to watch my granddaughter so she could get in some bowling practice for a class she was taking. I welcomed a chance to spend some quality time with my little toddler-aged grandchild. I didn't know then that helping my daughter take care of her business would allow her to help me take care of mine!

Unbeknownst to me, my older daughter liked to

catch the radio broadcast of a local pastor whenever she could. She said she liked his preaching because he chose one book of the Bible and then went straight through to the end—no "cherry-picking" or just taking out excerpts. When he started a new epistle, he introduced it by placing it in a framework of its cultural and historical context before beginning what was often a lengthy series.

After her bowling expedition that day, my daughter tuned in to his program on her drive home. The pastor was just starting to teach on 1st and 2nd Corinthians, two New Testament epistles written by the apostle Paul. He started by painting a backdrop of the Gentile converts living in pagan-dominated cities in the nation of Israel. Followers of the ancient pagan religions pressured those of other religions, including Christianity, to conform to their idolatry.

The pastor had pointed out pressures that a part of the early Church was having difficulty overcoming. The list included several beliefs and practices that can still be found in the mainstream churches of today that were born of that failure. Infant baptism was one! He said the belief that baptism saves came, not out of the Bible (as I had already learned), but from these ancient religions.

Although he apparently did not go into much detail, he explained that it was the goddess religions which, if we think of them at all, we think of as a part of the ancient world—certainly not today's world. He said these false religions were the source of astrology and infant baptism which would be very prevalent again in the end times.[3]

So, another string tied to infant baptism! This one would lead to astrology and the occult and straight into the heart of paganism!

This caused me to begin my search in earnest for the origins of infant baptism. Little did I know then that infant baptism *and the goddess religions* were tied together through a misinterpretation of the Noah and the Ark story!

---

[1] McClary, Judy M. *The Infant Baptism Saga: A Sinking Ship* (Minneapolis, MN: Magnolia Publications, 2014).

[2] Spitz, Lewis Spitz. *The Protestant Reformation* (Englewood Cliffs. NJ: Prentice-Hall, 1966), 97. Also Grimm, 166–167.

[3] From the Latin word, *occultus*, meaning hidden or secret – or, in this case, mysterious.

4
RE-IMAGINING THE CHURCH

Someone has said that a journey of a thousand miles begins with one small step. Enrolling in Bible school to discover the truth about infant baptism was my one small step. Throughout that first year, I was getting nowhere in my search to figure out the baptism issue though I asked many questions.

However, along the way, one of our instructors challenged us to research Martin Luther and the great Reformation in order to really know our church from the inside out. I grabbed onto this idea, thinking that such research might help me find the answers I needed. After all, Martin Luther was the one who had the revelation that we are saved through faith alone. Certainly his writings could be studied and they would explain how the belief that 'baptism saves' relates to his original revelation that salvation is by faith alone in the finished work of the cross.

Starting with the seemingly-disjointed topics of physical circumcision and the Reformation, I dove into my research with relish. It did not take long to realize that all was not as it seemed. The famous revelation that the young Martin Luther had received—that we are "saved by faith alone"—never even made it into the church he founded! And that was just the beginning!

Unraveling all the strings connected to infant baptism led me deep into the roots of the Reformation, to the legalization of the 'church' by Rome and—even before that—to its ties to the goddess-worshipping religions that came out of the Tower of Babel.

My church had asked for input from the congregation regarding its affiliation with the ELCA. I knew because of the information I was uncovering that they were going to need all the information they could get. So I shared my research with the pastors at our church so I wrote seven letters to our church as I researched infant baptism and Martin Luther.

Although I didn't hear anything back from my church, feedback would come from an entirely different source than I could have imagined. For suddenly, within a month after the last letter had gone out; an article unexpectedly showed up in our morning newspaper.

It was November 3, 1993, when the *Star Tribune* reported that a "RE-imagining" conference was being held the next day. This conference would be sponsored by infant baptism churches, including a $65,000 grant from the Presbyterian church (USA). The ELCA sent 313 people, including approximately twenty church staff from Chicago, Illinois, and the United Methodist's Division of Women designated the conference as their quadrennial spiritual renewal event for staff, even picking up the tab for the 52 directors and staff members who attended.[1]

RE-IMAGINING THE CHURCH

At this conference--Jesus Christ was not reverenced as one might expect at a conference sponsored by Christian churches—but a pagan goddess named Sophia![2] Instead, the leaders directed those present to pray to the goddess. "Our maker, Sophia," they prayed, "we are women in your image…with the hot blood of our wombs we give form to new life…."[3] They blessed Sophia with a communal blessing of rice milk and honey.

Throughout the conference, various leaders railed against Jesus Christ, with leader Delores Williams of Union Theological Seminary ranting against the atonement provided by His death on the Cross. She said, "I don't think we need a theory of atonement at all…I don't think we need folks hanging on crosses and blood dripping and weird stuff…we just need to listen to the god within."[4]

Mary Ann Lundy and female Bishop Forrest Stith, Presbyterian and Methodist co-chairs of the U.S. Committee for the Ecumenical Decade, called for radical theological surgery for the church. They insisted that women need to experience a revised theology based on their uniquely female experiences of the divine. Instead of seeking Biblical truth, the conference focus was on encouraging each woman to imagine her "own truth."

A World Council of Churches staff member from South India, Aruna Gnanadason,[5] protested Christian missionaries bringing the gospel to foreign lands. She led the conferees in anointing themselves with a red dot to recognize the "divine" in themselves. She said when she was a student it was her sign of protest against the missionary movement. Another speaker, this time from Korea, explained her view that "life-giving energy" can be drawn from nature when we "feel very tired and don't have any energy [of our own] to give"[6]

Homosexuality in the form of lesbianism was an honored theme throughout the conference as well. Melanie Morrison, Christian Lesbians Out Together (CLOUT), received a standing ovation as she celebrated the "miracle of being lesbian, Christian, and out!"[7]

Jane Spahr, lesbian clergywoman in Presbyterian Church USA claimed that her theology was first informed by making love to Coni, her lesbian partner. Speaker Mary Hunt said, "Imagine sex among friends as the norm."[8] Women and their female partners were called forward and given a standing ovation.

As the week of meetings progressed, I was stunned at what I read. *This goddess religion connection with infant baptism* was confirmation of the material I had uncovered in my research and written about in the letters to our pastors and elders.[9] I was shocked—but the affirmation of the accuracy of my research was there in black and white.

During the months of research, I waded through enough Mystery/goddess-religion filth to become uncomfortably familiar with the signs of the whore of Babylon busily at work—not just in the Old Testament but also beginning to unfold her handiwork in the New Testament Christian church. The signs were all there.

- Goddess-worship, usually accompanied by a pantheon of gods and goddesses
- Sexualization of 'worship', such as sexually-explicit (and sometimes violent) rituals, along with temple prostitutes and orgies of various kinds
- Androgyny in the priesthood, expressed as homosexuality in the populace
- Hypersexuality of the surrounding society in general, displayed in sexually-explicit arts & entertainment, and leading even to pedophilia and bestiality
- Use of religion to consolidate power, and persecution – sometimes including physical torture and murder – of those who can't be forced to worship the chosen god or goddess in the chosen *and legally-enforceable* way

It was there. As displayed at the "RE-imagining" conferences, it was *all* there! The goddess worship, the focus on sexuality, androgynous-homosexual themes, and the sexually-graphic "communion" language. The denouncing of devout believers who had risked their lives to tell others about a God who loves them; decrying the God of the Bible as an "abusive parent" who tortured His "obedient and trusting child."[10] A flat-out denial of the Blood's atoning power.

All the signs were there, just as they would be if my research into the infant baptism connection with the goddess religions and homosexuality were correct. I had a short-lived moment of relief that I had not been barking up the wrong tree or led astray as I had sent copies of my research to our home church. But my relief was short-lived. It was quickly followed by a deep sadness at what was happening to our denomination. Our denomination? *God's* Church, the Body of Christ!

According to the *Watchman Fellowship*, a self-identified Christian research and apologetics ministry, I was not the only church member taken by surprise at this betrayal of all the Bible teaches in regards to there being one God, that sin required a sinless Sacrifice for atonement, and that boundaries around sexuality are designed to keep marriages pure and able to provide a living analogy of the love that God has for His covenanted Bride.

As the Watchman Fellowship reported in its online journal, *Watchman Expositor*: "Many grass-roots members of the Presbyterian (PCUSA), Lutheran (ELCA) and United Methodist churches were also shocked when they heard about their denomination's participation in the themes and content of the conference which ranged from direct attacks on traditional Christian doctrine and the celebration of homosexuality, overt paganism, witchcraft, and New Age/Occult ritual."[11]

The *Jeremiah Project*, a youth-oriented organization founded by three United Methodist ministers in 1997, stated in its online article entitled "Re-Imagining Sophia" that the themes at the "RE-imagining" conference were intent on destroying traditional Christian faith. It included in its list these themes: adopting ancient pagan beliefs—rejecting Jesus' divinity and His atonement on the cross—creating a goddess in their own image—and affirming lesbian love-making.[12]

The goal of these conferences, according to the Jeremiah Project, was that Christ would be put down and the goddess Sophia raised up in churches and denominations everywhere.[13] Further research showed that, at the time of the "RE-imagining" conferences, there was already a seminary in Oklahoma that was dedicated to Sophia.[14]

The unabashed, stated mission of the *Sancta Sophia Seminary* is worship of Sophia. Along with its permanent staff that conducts the worship to Sophia, it recently added classes so they could restructure a master's degree program into a doctorate program. That way, they hope the extra credentialing will enable their graduates to qualify as chaplains in our nation's hospitals to spread the Sophia religion.[15]

I had started my quest with just a theoretical "Oh, no, what if...?" But it was no longer just empty words or stories from centuries past. Sophia groups and Sophia-awareness was the new direction of many of the women's groups in mainline churches—all traceable to the "RE-imagining" conferences.

As I looked around at the pile of books and notes that filled the makeshift office my dining room had become, I remembered the Scripture that says God uses the weak to confound the wise. Was it possible that a small, unknown layperson like myself needed to spread the word about the apostasy trying to enter many of our mainline denominational churches?

So I set about intensifying my research. I wanted to tie up any loose ends so that someone who might want to consider whether or not the baptism they received as an infant was really a part of the Gospel of Jesus Christ. They had the right to know if infant baptism really has the 'power' to save them or if Martin Luther and the Roman Catholic church had led them astray.

My intent was to get the material I had uncovered into the hands of anyone who might want the opportunity to consider it for, ten years after the first "RE-imagining" conference took place in 1993, the Witherspoon planners announced they were closing their offices. The 2003 conference would be their last and they would set back and watch the seeds they had planted sprout and flourish.

> The Re-Imagining leadership has decided that following this celebration of all that has been done over the past decade, they will close their office by the end of the year, with the confidence that the seeds generated by the movement *will continue to spread and flourish.*[16]

So now, several years later, plenty of time has passed to allow us to assess the fruit of those conferences. Were the seeds the Witherspoon folk planted successful in changing the Church?

And did the seeds indeed take hold and flourish in the churches that sponsored the "RE-imagining" conferences?

[1] *Washington Post.* June 4, 1994. C
[2] *Star Tribune: "The divine redefined"* by Martha Sawyer Allen, staff writer, 1Bw. 11-3-93.
[3] Katherine A. Kersten, *Lutheran Commentator.* "God in Your Mirror?" May/June, 1994, Vol. 7. No. 6. pp.1, 7.
[4] Ibid.
[5] www.biblicalwitness.org/uncloseting.htm
[6] Cloud, David. *The Way of Life Literature, Inc.*, www.wayoflife.org/database/wcc.html, quoting the AFA Journal, Feb. 1994.
[7] Kersten, Katherine A. *Lutheran Commentator.* "God in Your Mirror?" May/June, 1994, Vol. 7. No. 6. pp.1, 7.
[8] www.nplainste.org/html/world_council_of_churches.html
[9] *Seven Letters to the Infant Baptism Church: A Layperson Speaks Out.* www.magnoliapubl.com
[10] Mollenkott, Virginia, conference speaker and contributor to the *New International Version* of the Bible, according to the online article, *The World Council of Churches.* David Cloud, The Way of Life Literature, Inc. www.wayoflife.org/database/wcc.html
[11] Branch, Craig. "Re-imaging God," *Watchman Expositor*, Vol. 11, No. 5, 1994. www.watchman.org/reltop/reimagin.htmhttp://www.watchman.org/reltop/reimagin.htm
[12] http://touchstonemag.com/archives/article.php?id=10-02-024-f
[13] "Re-Imagining Sophia," *The Jeremiah Project*, www.jeremiahproject.com/prophecy/feminist4.html
[14] http://www.jeremiahproject.com/prophecy/feminist4.html
[15] Sancta Sophia Seminary website: www.sanctasophia.org/
[16] www.witherspoonsociety.org/03-may/reimagining_2003.htm

5
RECYCLING SOPHIA

Many have looked at the fruit of the "RE-imagining" conferences and realized that the Witherspoon planners were indeed successful in changing the sponsoring denominations—just as they set out to do.

Unfortunately, when one attempts to change or add to the word of God, they are attempting to desecrate the holiness of God. In the Zondervan NASB Exhaustive Concordance, it records the fact that there So once again, chants and harmonious alleluias could be heard as they worshiped Sophia at the thirteenth annual *Voices of Sophia* breakfast during the 220th General Assembly of the Presbyterian church that was held Tuesday, July 3, 2012.

The event was sponsored by *Presbyterian Voices for Justice*. Sylvia Thorson-Smith, new co-moderator, reflected on the Re-Imagining Conferences of a decade ago. She suggested new ways to move the church forward, asserting that God can be imagined and re-imagined by many names, including Sophia."[1]

Those who attempt to make a goddess out of the New Testament Greek word *Sophia* have confused it with the Old Testament Hebrew word *chakam* which

31

means wisdom.[2] The *Greek-English Lexicon* notes that the Greek word simply means *"mental excellence...and implies goodness."*[3]

In the Old Testament, however, *chakam* does have female imagery displayed as a quality needful for both male and female. One example is Proverbs 7 which states, "Say unto wisdom, Thou art my sister; and call understanding thy kinswoman: That they may keep thee from the strange [sexually immoral] woman, from the stranger which flattereth with her words." (Proverbs 7:4-5 KJV)

A further study of the Hebrew word *chakam,* for those interested in accuracy, can be found in the Book of Proverb and is translated *wisdom.* It is found in the Old Testament and ultimately refers to Jesus Christ who had not yet been manifested. So the imagery connected with wisdom is actually taken from the Old Testament not from *the word Sophia* found in the New Testament.

It was the Greeks who originally coined the word *"sophism"*[4] for what was described as a group of ne'er do wells that used their mental acumen for the purpose of deception—whether of people, in business, or in religion. The word denoted sophisticated deception. It was first used to explain the twisting of words one may use in rhetorical speeches to deceive one's listener.

Sophism was a philosophy that began about the fifth century B.C. A cult following of sophists was led by an Italian woman named Julia Domna who was an important figure in the late second century/early third century. She was strongly against Christianity, encouraging neoplatonic philosophy and popularizing the sophist rhetoric found in Philostratus' *Lives of the Sophists* and *Life of Apollonius of Tyana*.

Prolific sophist author, Porphyry, wrote fifteen books in which he sought to bring Christian doctrine into disrepute including the incarnation of Christ.[5] Through his writings, a Christianized version of philosophy/sophism developed which almost destroyed Christianity.[6]

Sophism gained entrance into parts of the early church when a virtuous Christian woman named Sophia was venerated with her three daughters. They are portrayed in history as remaining faithful to God during severe persecution. From this incident, a Sophia cult emerged whose followers venerated her for her wisdom, even assigning the date December 25th to commemorate her holy Ascension into heaven. This date was copied from the Roman Catholic Church who had already assigned that date as the birthday of Jesus Christ, stealing it from pagan sun worship.[7]

As the sophia cult expanded, mythology grew up around the godly woman whose name was Sophia and assigned her the position of goddess. Myths emerged that gave her higher spiritual authority than Jesus Christ. The Witherspoon Society seized upon the name 'Sophia' to propagate the idea that Christ's spiritual wisdom and authority emanated from her rather than His being the Son of God.[8]

A version of Sophism was widespread in the Church of Rome in the days of the Emperor Constantine. At that time, an unconverted priest named Arius maintained that Jesus Christ was not God but was of the same substance as Zeus, Hercules or Baal. The Church fathers asked a reluctant Constantine to call the Nicene Council. At this council, the Nicene Creed was crafted to deal with this attack against the deity of Christ.[9]

Sophia is also the name of a Gnostic figure that is central to the Secret Symbols of the Roscrucians. Gnostics were people who 'knew.' They believed knowledge—not repentance and faith in Christ—was the way to gain favor with God. Rosicrucianism was an ancient and feared occult organization during the 16th and 17th centuries, with remnants remaining today.[10]

One example of the recycling of the sophism heresy over the centuries that is easy to research is the seventeenth century revival that began when Jane Leade, a Universalist, began a campaign to bring sophism back into the church. She wrote of visions and dialogues she said came from Sophia.[11]

Leade, similarly, was influenced by a 16th century German mystic named Jakob Bohme, author of *The Way to Christ.*[12] This heresy endangered the faith of believers during those centuries and it was not until the 18th and early 19th centuries, that religious opinion once again turned against the Sophists who were thoroughly exposed as charlatans.

Now this heresy is coming to the forefront again as a result of the decade of "RE-imagining" conferences held between 1993 and 2003. Bishop William Cannon states this most recent re-emergence of

Sophism can be traced, at least in part, to a book written by two United Methodist ministers and a Roman Catholic.[13] It includes worship services to Sophia and contains liturgies that support worship of the goddess.

Thus the sophism heresy has recycled over and over during the past two thousand years, and is again attempting to worm its way into the Church through the efforts of the Witherspoon Society. Its sinister purpose is to undermine Jesus' authority and cause people to distrust the Atonement provided by His death and resurrection.

---

[1] www.pcusa.org/news/2012/7/7/voices-sophia-breakfast-thorson-smith-reflects-bac/

[2] *Zondervan NASB Exhaustive Concordance*, 1391. (Zondervan, Grand Rapids, MI. ©1981.)

[3] Vine, W.E. *Vine's Expository Dictionary of Old & New Testament Words.* Nashville, TN. Thomas Nelson, Inc., 1997. 414..

[4] www.iep.utm.edu/sophists/ www.iep.utm.edu/sophists/ www.merriam-webster.com/dictionary/sophist

[5] Davies, J. G. *The Early Christian Church.* New York: Holt, Rinehart, and Winston, 1965. 113.

[6] Dake, Finis Jennings. *Dake's Annotated Reference Bible.* Lawrencevill, GA. Dake Publishing, Inc. 1999. 50.

[7] www.religioustolerance.org/xmas_sel.htm The March of Sophia," www.chalcedon.edu

[8] I John 4:1-3

[9] Davies, J. G. *The Early Christian Church.* New York: Holt, Rinehart, and Winston, 1965. 176.

[10] www.crcsite.org/ViriginSophia.htm

[11] en.wikipedia.org/wiki/Sophia_(wisdom) [Caitlin Matthews, *Sophia: Goddess of Wisdom* (London: Madala, 1991) ISBN OO44405901]
[12] Ibid. [Jakob Bohme, The Way to Christ (1622) [6]
[13] www.goodnewsmag.org/library/articles/cannon-ma94.htm

6

CHICKEN OR THE EGG?

Philip G. Davis, author of *Goddesses Unmasked,* blames the thinkers of the Enlightenment Era of the 1700's for setting the background for today's interest in goddess worship found in many mainline denominational churches.

As you may know, thinkers of the "Enlightenment" Era believed there was a natural order in the universe and set about uncovering it. They established a method known as the *modern scientific method*. They believed that with careful observation and experimental testing, they could generate a rational explanation for any piece of data they could compile. So focused were they that their detractors in the following Romantic Era accused them of being cold and calculating and of narrowing human emotions to chemical reactions in the brain.[1]

The thinkers of the Enlightenment Era did not limit their focus to science's explanation of the universe. They also used their newfound influence to tear down the Church and Jesus Christ. They lumped the misdeeds of the Roman Catholic church with the teachings of Jesus Christ and were scathing in their attacks and attempts to tear down Christianity.

They were successful in discrediting not just the Roman Catholic church but all churches. As the era of Enlightenment faded and Romanticism emerged, the only people who remained willing to be associated with the Church was a small, non-influential remnant. The rest wanted nothing to do with religion although that remnant is slowly increasing in numbers.

Those from the romantic era wanted to participate in spirituality, but they wanted to be turned onto something other than Christianity. At a time when "the church" and "Christianity" seemed to be exemplified" by the excesses of the Roman Catholic church, they saw spirituality during that time period as shrouded in error and misconception. In a word, they embraced *neopaganism*, a version stemming from the pagan religions popular during the time of Christ.

In the ensuing years, the avant-garde among them took to meeting their spiritual needs with pseudoreligions. Many were pantheists, believing God was in everything and everyone. If anything, they were mystics inspired by the eastern religions. The rituals and ceremonies of these religions were designed to encourage spiritual as well as interpersonal bonding with other women and nature.

Wicca, a forerunner of today's *Sophism* revival seen in the Protestant churches that sponsored the "RE-imagining" conferences, is a new incarnation of an old religion. It embraces the ropes of ancient witchcraft, but is actually a contemporary form that only dates back to the 1950's.[2]

Wiccans often have god/goddess or priest/ priestess leadership couples, but the female is always the powerful one. Wiccans also have all-female covens; as well as covens of those seeking to recover magic formulas practiced by ancient Egyptians, Norse, or Celts—all are part of today's neopaganism.

The "second-wave" of feminists after the 1960's was also drawn to neopaganism. They attacked Christianity by launching a biblical-wording campaign, bullying biblical scholars into making changes in words identifying gender of both God and humans. Although, as scholars, they likely understood the nuances of the Hebrew language, they chose to disregard these nuances in which feminine terms refer only to females; and masculine terms are used for either of two categories: (1) male and (2) 'all inclusive.'

Feminists successfully began an outcry against the Bible that produced first a change from "gender equity" (equal treatment of both males and females) to "gender supremacy" in which the female was raised to an almost goddess-like persona. By the 1970's, books began to be published that touted feminine superiority with goddess spirituality soon following.

In answer to the question, "Who are these goddess worshipers?" A portrait comes forth that shows today's neopagans are different from witches of the past. While previous purveyors of witchcraft were shown as a disgruntled, poverty-stricken demographic stereotyped by Halloween posters; today they are pictured as mainly white women in their 30's and 40's. Most are disappointed, middle class, reasonably educated women who feel a sense of anger with society at large; and are especially alienated from Judaism and Christianity.

The black church, on the other hand, has tried to distance themselves from the feminist movement.[3] While white feminist theologians denigrate the institutional church and advise women to abandon their mainstream beliefs, Linda E. Thompson, Lutheran School of Theology in Chicago, Illinois, does not wish to be identified with them. She says, "For African American women, the black church has been the central historical institution which has helped their families to survive."[4]

She says that while they do not hesitate to critique the black church, most black women embrace Christianity. For this reason, she takes the approach that they do not want to be aligned with white feminists; saying they prefer to call themselves 'womanists.'

The Vatican, for their part, feels they have plenty to worry about in this area. Not only are they dealing with child abuse from their homosexual clergy, they are also worried over the sharp increase of goddess worship they see in their church's community of nuns. As early as 1993, the year goddess worship was introduced to mainline denominational churches at the "RE-imagining" conference; Pope John Paul II was already letting his worries about the rise of goddess worship in their church be known.

At the time, he warned American bishops to be on the lookout to keep goddess worship out of their dioceses. He told them not to support conferences such as the *"Celebrate Women"* conferences that were springing up. He said they were polarizing men and

CHICKEN OR THE EGG?

women and not willing to uphold Catholic doctrine.[5]

According to a recent statement from the Vatican, this subject continues to have the Roman Catholic church on high alert. Within a month after taking office, the new pope, Pope Francis, went on record that he considered a 'program of reform' for American nuns a priority.[6]

This was not a new direction for the Catholic church. Pope Francis said he was merely "reaffirming the findings" of the Vatican investigation into goddess worship and that he planned to continue the "program of reform" started by his predecessors, John Paul II and Pope Emeritus Benedict XVI.[7]

But does this mean that the Vatican is against the goddess worship that is spreading among their nuns even while seeming to discredit New Age? Unfortunately, it does not. While warning nuns to pull back from the New Age and the goddess religions, Catholic clergy remain zealous for the Virgin Mary calling her both "Queen of Heaven" and "Mother of God," titles that continue to be used in the mystery religions for goddesses such as Ishtar, Isis, Astarte, Asheroth and other goddesses but are also unabashedly used for Catholicism's own 'goddess,' the Madonna and son.[8]

Meanwhile, many of the infant baptism sponsors of the "RE-imagining" conferences, the Presbyterian Church (USA), the United Methodist Church, the Episcopalian church and the ELCA (Evangelical Lutheran Church in America)—continue to expand the Sophia movement with the Witherspoon planners of those conferences merging with 'Voices of Sophia."

Thus the thread of goddess worship that even their leaders may have been surprised to discover is found hidden in the goddess religion roots of infant baptism!

---

[1] Davies, Philip G. *Goddesses Unmasked*. 14.
[2] Ibid. 19.
[3] www.blackandchristian.com/articles/academy/thomas-05-01.shtml
[4] Ibid. "Womanist Theology, Epistemology, and a New Anthropological Paradigm, Part II.
[5] Davis, Philip G. 28.
[6] www.traditioninaction.org/RevolutionPhotos/A101rcDancingNuns.htm
[7] www.religionnews.com/2013/04/15/pope-francis-orders-overhaul-of-u-s-nuns-to-continue/
[8] israelsmessiah.com/religions/new_age.htm

7
A PATH TO THE PULPIT

If the sin of the Witherspoon Society's plan for the "RE-imagining " conferences was to acclimate sponsoring churches to accept goddess worship in place of the worship of Jesus Christ, they got their point across.

Their second objective was surely acclimating these same churches to the possibility of sexually-active homosexual clergy in their pulpits. The question about whether that succeeded hardly needs to be addressed either—they were very successful in their goal.

At the time, most members of the churches that openly sponsored the "RE-imagining" conferences were shocked to hear about the conference themes and its content.[1] But as time went on, it was like putting a frog in a pan of cold water and setting it on a slow burner—they slowly grew accustomed.

At the time of the last conference, in 2003, the Witherspoon Society stated that, following the celebration of all they had accomplished during the past decade at the June meeting, they would close their office by the end of the year. They said they were confident that the seeds they had planted would continue to spread and flourish. Now we have to ask ourselves, what was the fruit that they believed would come to pass in the Christian church as a result of their agenda in the "RE-imagining" conferences?

First of all, we have to affirm their effectiveness in changing the Protestant churches that openly sponsored the conferences.

- ELCA (Evangelical Lutheran Church in America)
- Presbyterian Church (USA)
- Episcopalian Church
- United Methodist church

The attempt to gain acceptance of the gay agenda in the Church, something for which the average member of the Protestant church was unprepared in 1991, began to move forward after the "REimagining: conferences. At that time, no church denomination openly condoned sodomite clergy.

A group from the ELCA Lutheran church called *Lutherans' Concerned* formed and they began to study sexual orientation and promote understanding and acceptance of gays and lesbians as full members of the Lutheran church even though there were no church laws denying them that privilege. Only later would it be understood that their agenda was not to become full members (they already had those privileges) but to rule church congregations as fully-practicing homosexuals.

At first the ELCA Lutheran church asserted that the Biblical understanding which this church affirms is that the normative settings for sexual intercourse is marriage. Practicing homosexuals would be excluded from the ordain ministry. This would change.

- In 1991, the ELCA punished a Berkeley seminary student who urged Lutherans to study the homosexual issue on their own. The church council suspended his financial support and he was forced to leave seminary.

- That same year, the biannual *Church wide Assembly* voted to *"affirm gay and lesbian people, as individuals created by God."* The church, however, refused to bless their committed relationships and did not ordain them nor allow them to be clergy.

- In 1993, a committee of the ELCA prepared a draft which stated that the Bible did not condemn homosexual relationships. They received 21,000 responses from angry church members decrying this as apostasy.

- In 1994, the church avoided acting on any homosexual resolutions by putting it off until its 1999 assembly.

- In 1995, the ELCA voted to affirm homosexual and gay people but refused to ordain them or bless same sex unions.

- In 1996, the ELCA's *Southwestern Texas Synod* defeated a resolution which would have allowed lesbians and gays as clergy.
- In 1999, the ELCA banned sexually-active gays and lesbians from ordination.

In August of 2009, the whole world watched with bated breath as the gay clergy controversy took over newspapers and magazines to report the actions of the ELCA as it gathered at a conference to decide the official position their denomination would take regarding the gay lifestyle.

---

[1] www.watchman.org/reltop/reimagin.htm

8

IS THE CHURCH AT RISK?

It was sunny that Wednesday afternoon in downtown Minneapolis. The date was August 19, 2009. People were out and about, taking care of business. Church members at the downtown Central Lutheran Church were preparing to serve a beautiful, outdoor dinner to honor delegates attending the ELCA Churchwide Assembly next door.

Suddenly, from out of nowhere, a tornado appeared in the midst of blue skies overhead. It came barreling down and headed for Central Lutheran church headquarters and those attending the Churchwide Assembly.

Like a trajectory shot from a rocket, the tornado headed straight for the cross sitting on a high and lofty steeple above Central Lutheran church. It blasted the cross from its moorings, leaving it dangling upside down by a cable.

But it was not done. It dumped the heavy pots and pans and dinner fixings on Third Street a couple blocks over before heading right to the top of the Minneapolis Convention Center next door. What, you may ask, *was going on* at the Center that had caused such a stir? The Church Council of the Evangelical Lutheran Church in America was having a week-long assembly to debate and vote on several issues that had become controversial within the denomination.

The centerpiece of the convention came in two parts. First, they were to vote on a proposed social statement on human sexuality. They were deciding on whether to override the Bible's ban on homosexuality and officially accept it as a lifestyle choice.

The second proposal was their planned vote on whether to allow sexually-active homosexuals to be ordained as clergy in ELCA churches. The first was to be decided that afternoon and the second, two days later, on Friday.

The week had gotten off to a rocky start. Someone had proposed that the gay-clergy vote should require a two-thirds majority to pass as had been required of other, lesser shifts, in church policy. That proposal was voted down. This left the social statement vote—which already required a supermajority—as the only real obstacle on the path to the ELCA (Evangelical Lutheran Churches in America) ordaining practicing homosexuals.

Both the debate and the vote on homosexuality had been scheduled for that afternoon but the day was so beautiful and the sunshine so inviting that none of the matters seemed too pressing. After all, the homosexuality matter being voted on was merely a *social* statement. There was even talk of cancelling the afternoon sessions. Many of the delegates, believing a decision to postpone had been made, left for the day's luncheon.

But, lo and behold! Having thinned the herd, the

remaining delegates chose to stay and decide right then the issue of homosexuality in the ELCA. The gay world was ecstatic. Those who'd propagated the "RE-imagining" conference had finally gotten what they were after—the go-ahead to venture into a coveted area where they'd never *officially* been allowed before—the pulpit of the Christian church.

Thus, the monumental shift, steering the ELCA away from nearly two thousand years of Christian church that was *supposed* to require the votes of at least practice two-thirds of the church delegates, was passed instead by two-thirds of the delegates who were *present at the moment of the vote*. The resolution passed by one vote.

But what about the tornado? Having knocked the cross off the steeple of the host-church and strewing the fancy dinner preparations all over the ground, the tornado then headed for the Minneapolis Convention Center next door where the vote was being taken. Though the cross and steeple have since been reunited, no one aware of the proceedings taking place next door at the Minneapolis Convention Center will soon forget the impression left behind that God's anger had been suddenly and strikingly provoked.

For it was at the moment of the vote—*that the tornado left the church area and headed next door to the convention center where it tore up the roof and dumped dirty water and debris from the storm into the opening before it departed.*

So, what about the tornado? Had God voted, too? And, if so, is the Church risking further correction from the hand of its long-suffering Father?

9
CHECKING THE FRUIT

If, as the Bible states, you can tell a tree by its fruit, we need to dig deeper into what happened at the "RE-imagining" conferences. While it is true that the last conference happened in 2003, it gives us plenty of opportunity to see things more clearly through the lenses of time.

One of the single biggest consequences of the declining influence of the church has been a rise in neopaganism—a spirituality that returns to the goddess religions prominent in the Roman Empire at the time of Christ. They are just another term for the mystery religions warned about in the Bible where a rise in popularity would signal the end of the age.

The end times are a time of justice being meted out, yet it is also a favorable time in that there is plenty of time to repent and get right with God—the question is—has man gone so far that *he doesn't want to repent anymore?*

In an article in USA TODAY, a reporter holds out little hope for the mainline denominational churches that dot the landscape of most of Europe. The waning influence of religion also has brought a change in attitudes and laws on issues such as divorce, abortion, and gay marriage.

Brian Kenny, a student studying psychotherapy and counseling at Dublin's Business School states in the same article that he doesn't go to church anymore. He says, "I don't know one person who does. Fifteen years ago, I didn't know one person who didn't."[1]

Mary Haugh, elderly widow, agrees with him. In the once religious nation of Ireland, she has gone to Mass seven days a week for most of her 79 years. She is saddened by what she calls the apostasy she sees, flatly stating that, "It's a Godless society. Materialism has taken over... It has replaced God."[2]

Ireland is not an exception in Western Europe. Pope Benedict XVI commented to Italian priests that "The so-called traditional churches look like they are dying." He said, "There's no longer evidence for a need of God, even less of Christ."

Though many Europeans consider themselves Christian versus, say, Muslim, few attend services and the majority of those that do, are elderly. A struggle to regain souls and the need to revive the Roman Catholic church is among the main reasons Pope Benedict, a German cardinal, was chosen to succeed Pope John Paul II. British Cardinal Cormac Murphy-O'Connor told the *Associated Press* shortly after Pope Benedict was elected, that, "Nobody is better informed than Pope Benedict on the European scene and the secularism of Europe."[3]

Notwithstanding their attempt at revitalization, not even one priest was ordained in Dublin in 2005.

When this downward trend began varies from country to country. Wars and revolutions have always played a decisive role in shaping faith in Europe. The spread of religion and the conversion of the masses often were bloody affairs—from the Crusades and the papal wars to the Spanish Inquisition and the Protestant Reformation—uprisings against ruling religious power was often brutal, as has been the 30-year conflict in Northern Ireland pitting Protestants against Catholics.

In attempts to regain the loyalty of their members, perhaps the Catholic Church should be looking at the gay sexual scandals as at least partial reason for the decline in interest among young males of an age to enter the priesthood. This may also hold the solution to the question of why the nation of Ireland is currently in sharp decline in church attendance as well as the reason why so few children have a desire to be men and women of the cloth, unlike past generations.

Government investigations are reaching into previously secret church records in Ireland and are uncovering decades of child abuse by the priests in Catholic-run schools, workhouses, and orphanages. The Dublin probe has unearthed a cover-up attempt by Irish bishops to hide the documentation of the raping of thousands of boys and girls who also suffered beatings and mental cruelty at the hands of Catholic religious orders.

> "This is the second major government-ordered report this year exploring how and

why Irish authorities permitted widespread abuse of boys and girls at the hands of the Catholic Church throughout most of the 20th century, the gravest scandal in the history of independent Ireland."[4]

Even Pope Benedict XVI is under suspicion of having covered up priest abuse of Catholic children. According to a recent Wall Street Journal article, the Pope met with a German archbishop to discuss the more than 100 cases dating back to the 1970s which are under investigation in the pope's former diocese of Munich-Freising. This has become a crucial test of his papal legacy as cases involving sexual abuse by priests have strained financial resources in dioceses in the United States, Australia and other countries.[5]

The Vatican protected Pope Benedict from what they denounced as an aggressive attempt to drag him into the spreading scandals. At the same time, they admitted that more than 3,000 cases of child sexual abuse by priests have come to light in the past decade with only 20 percent being brought to trial in Vatican courts.[6]

As scandals over homosexual priests continue to spread both here and abroad, supporters of Pope Benedict tell of an incident in Mexico where they believe he tried to take action in a case before he was pope. The Mexican case recounted decades of sexual abuse by one of the most powerful priests in the Roman Catholic church. He asked to look into the case and then halted the inquiry; telling a Mexican bishop, "It isn't prudent."[7]

According to the *Washington Post,* correspondence released as late as the 1990s between the Holy See and Wisconsin bishops shows that Rome failed to defrock a priest who had molested as many as 200 deaf boys even though bishops contacted the doctrinal office headed by Cardinal Joseph Ratzinger, Pope Benedict XVI.[8]

The Vatican has since issued long-awaited rules dealing with clergy sex abuse. The Vatican's new ruling, when one takes a closer look, equates the actions of those who ordain women clergy with priests who molest the mentally ill or use child pornography.[9] It does not address the issue of their clergy's sexual abuse of children. Instead, the Roman church contends that their actions have been *"taken out of context."*

Today, since his resignation, he is known as Pope Emeritus Benedict but while he was still leader of the giant church, he attempted to lead the Roman Catholic faithful to take a stand against gay marriage, hoping to keep it from being approved in state-by-state referendums. Perhaps better than other organizations, in their attempt to cover up the burgeoning secrets of priest sexual abuse of children, they understand the monstrous problems that homosexuality in the ranks have produced within their church.

The Roman Catholic church is under an avalanche of child abuse cases that threaten to bankrupt the once-wealthy church.

---

[1] Noelle Knox. *USA TODAY.* 8-11-05. p1, 2A.

[2] Ibid.
[3] Ibid. (*Associated Press*. British cardinal cormac Murphy-O'Connor.)
[4] www.foxnews.cokkm/story/0,2933,577106,00.html. 11-29-09. *Associated Press*. Dublin.
[5] *The Wall Street Journal* by Stacy Meichtry and David Crawford. A10. 3-12-10.
[6] *Star Tribune*, Minneapolis, Mn. New Services. A14. 3-14-10.
[7] *New York Times* by D. J. Wakin and J. C. McKinley, Jr. [Star Tribune. 5-3-2010.]
[8] www.washingtonpost.com/wpdyn/content/article/2010/03/26/AR2010032604897_2.html
[9] *Washington Post* by Wm. Wan [Star Tribune. 7-16-2011.]

10
DELAYED JUSTICE

The issue refuses to go away. In a neighboring small town newspaper, the *St. Cloud Times,* a recent article was titled, *Lawsuit: Man was Abused by Priest.*[1]

In the *Associated Press* article, a civil lawsuit was filed in St. Paul by a man who claims he was sexually abused by a priest 40 years ago. He was only now able to come forward because of a recent action of the Minnesota Legislature that loosened the statute of limitations on sexual crimes.

"Doe 1," is the label given the 51-year old gentleman identified in court records who seeks at least $50,000 in damages—a pittance for the emotional and physical harm done when he was a young teenage altar boy. This was the first lawsuit filed under the new law signed into effect by Governor Mark Dayton. It cancels the past six-year civil statute of limitations for victims of childhood sexual abuse.

Residents are up in arms against the Catholic church in this small Midwestern city. They are taking it very personally for, according to the lawsuit, Father Thomas Adamson 'engaged in unpermitted sexual contact' with the boy while he was working in a trusted position at St. Thomas Aquinas parish in St.

Paul Park that allowed him to have 'unlimited access' to many of their children.

The lawsuit accuses the Archdiocese of St. Paul and Minneapolis as well as the Diocese of Winona of knowing—or they should have known—that Adamson had 'sexually molested dozens of boys, had admitted to molesting boys, and that he had committed offenses at almost every parish he served." The lawsuit labels them as 'public nuisances' because even then they refused to release the names of forty-six 'credibly accused child-molesting priests.'[2]

They are also labeled as 'co-defendants' in the case along with the offending priest because, as pointed out by the St. Paul attorney for the plaintiff, Catholic kids remain in great peril because parents and law officers do not know who these offenders are, but the archdiocese and dioceses do. He seeks a court order to demand the release if these names 'so kids in our community and across Minnesota can be better protected."

The attorney went on to state that the Twin Cities' archdiocese and Winona Diocese's "repeated abuse and sordid saga of cover-up" was spread over 15 job assignments in southern Minnesota and the Twin Cities between 1958 and 1985. He said at least fourteen of those transfers were made by church officials as a result of specific accusations that came forth accusing Father Adamson of rape and molestation of children yet he was not released from the priesthood until 2007. Neither was the priest barred from diocese parishes and schools until 2012 when an outcry by newspapers and online sources began demanding the accountability of the Roman Catholic church and hoping to force them to expose the names of clergy who molest boys and girls.

We watch with bated breath to see how judges rule in the numerous lawsuits pending throughout the United States and overseas. It was to Minnesota Governor Mark Dayton's credit that he recently signed a bill into law that allowed adults sexually violated years ago by predator priests to get justice in the courtroom.

It is important that victims see their abusers judged and sentenced for the crimes perpetrated on the body, soul and spirit of their inner child. Those molested as children must not be shunted aside!

---

[1] *St. Cloud Times.* www.sctimes.com. STATE. Thursday, May 30, 2013, 5B.
[2] Ibid.

11
PAGE FROM AN ANCIENT PLAYBOOK

Homosexuality in religion is not a new phenomenon. It was common practice for ancient pagan religions. One example was in the Roman Empire during the time of Jesus.

Today there are large and expensive spas and hotels in the valleys around Rome where temples to false gods and goddesses once stood. Although the temples are now empty ruins, worship once took place amidst a backdrop of hot mineral springs with billowing sulfuric smoke that rolled forth from the holes in cave floors.

The economy in this region benefited commercially from the magnificent goddess temples in their midst. Foreign caravans made special pilgrimages to "worship" at the altars of such goddesses as the virgin Diana or Aphrodite.

While the priesthood of these religions was forced to be celibate, cult prostitution flourished. Both male and female prostitution was rampant within the temples. The promiscuous sexuality and lewd fertility rites performed within them debased the structure of family life. Even married women served as cult prostitutes with virgin daughters conscripted to serve the visiting caravans at least once before they could be married."[1]

Purity, however, was demanded of the men who served in the position of priest to the goddesses of the ancient pagan religions because of their respect for their divine idol. Celibacy was required of the priest to prove their loyalty to the goddess, the priest had to become sexless—the term for this was *androgynous*—a body in which both male and female reside. This was a drive to revert back to the androgynous state of Adam, the first man, prior to the time when God created a helpmate for him. God originally formed Adam in this state but He later separated them into two genders 'because it was not good' that man should be alone.[2]

Paganism, however, desired a return to Adam's original androgynous state in their attempt to retain both masculinity and femininity in one body. In their attempt to do this, the pagan priesthood willingly submitted to castration by the goddess' representative to prove their devotion to the goddess.[3]

What hasn't been so clear in the past is what the androgynous priest received back from the goddess? He had willingly cast aside his human sexual identity. Now, according to *The Journal of the Evangelical Theological Society,* the exchange has become clearer. Having proven his devotion to the goddess by emptying himself of his sexual nature, the pagan priesthood was now capable of receiving unlimited amounts of the demon power associated with the goddess religions.

Nor was this combination of sexuality and spirituality unusual in the pagan religions. According to theologian, F.F. Bruce, the co-mixture of religiosity and sexuality was found in pagan religions as a matter of course.[4]

---

[1] www.en.wikipedia.org/wiki/Sacred_prostitution

[2] Genesis 2:15-25

[3] Armstrong & Armstrong. web7.epnet.com Beard, M.; North J. et al. *Religions of Rome*. (Cambridge University Press. Cambridge, UK. © 2004.) 210-211.

[4] Bruce, F. F. *The International Bible Commentary with the NIV*. Grand Rapids, MI: Zondervan Publishing House, 1979, 5.

12
A SECRET & TERRIBLE CONSPIRACY

I had my two questions nearly answered. Our church had answered the second question for me-- they had chosen to leave the ELCA because of the ungodly choices it was making in refuting biblical instruction and accepting the homosexual lifestyle. So, as inferred in the *draft on human sexuality,* the "RE-imagining" conferences had embraced homosexuals in the pulpit but our church had boldly chosen to embrace the Bible's teaching.

The other question, however, required more research. Our church had not chosen to reject infant baptism even though there were no actual examples of infant baptism in the Bible but required smoke-and-mirrors (see Appendix i) to continue with it. And who could blame them? With a doctrine that well-embedded in the church doctrine of 1.2 billion Catholics and many of the more than half-a-billion Protestants that attend infant baptism churches--who could blame them for 'keeping up appearances' and taking the easy way out?

Nonetheless, I had begun to wonder what was in the roots of the churches that sponsored the "RE-imagining" conferences for the Bible says you can tell a tree by its fruit. I wondered if the fact that all the main sponsors of these churches were infant baptism churches was significant and so I turned back to my original question on the origins of infant baptism.

There are few who might guess that if the origins of infant baptism could be uncovered at all, it would lead back to the time of Noah and the Ark. In fact, there are those who scoff at the possibility of a major occurrence such as a flood covering the whole world. But there is much scientific evidence that such a flood did really occur; even remnants of the ark have been sighted and procured.[1] Archeologists dig up fossils showing the sudden demise of animals caught in a state of catastrophe as rain began to fall.

A professor at a nearby college routinely scoffed at Christianity in his *"Developing a Philosophy of Life"* class. Noah and the flood story was one of his major targets. The Bible, he would say at the beginning of each semester, is just a book of myths like those found in all other world religions. According to him, the Bible was nothing more than folklore. He pointed out that almost all world religions and literature contain some version of a flood story which, in his worldview, made Noah nothing special.

I was in class one day when he began expounding this opinion. A new student's hand shot up. "Sir," the question was asked, "have you considered the possibility that the flood story might be true—that where there is so much smoke—maybe there really was a fire?"

The prepared student then began to read a footnote from the Amplified Bible. It said that in 1606, a man named P. Jansen of Hoorn, Holland, had produced a model of the ark fashioned after the pattern God gave Noah in Genesis 6:14-16.[2]

The discovery was made that the pattern for the ark that God gave Noah was wonderfully seaworthy. The vessel was light, waterproof, comfortable, well-ventilated and perfectly planned to be large enough to accommodate the original land animals as well as four couples for the duration of the flood and the drying out period that followed. In fact, it could carry one-third more cargo than any other ship of similar cubical proportions.

According to the *Registry of Shipping, World Almanac*,[3] Jansen's model of the ark revolutionized shipbuilding and the world's navies. After 1609 when the model was made, ocean-going ships began to be patterned after the biblical rendering of God's blueprint given Noah to build the ark, for it was beautifully designed and "well-adapted for floating."

The design of the world's ships only changed again later after vessels became engine-driven and needed a contour designed to be more conducive to speed—a matter of no particular concern to Noah. The professor conceded, and wondered why no one had ever told him that before.

The fact that the biblical rendering of the Noah and the Ark story is accurate is no surprise to Bible readers who have long believed that Noah was a real human being and that a flood covered the earth in his day. The Bible teaches that Noah alone was righteous of all the people who were alive on the earth at that time.[4] So he was righteous in the eyes of God long before God gave him the instructions that would allow him to build the ark that saved him and his family from destruction when the big flood came.

Elsewhere in the Bible, Noah is called "the preacher."[5] It is easy to picture him, the one righteous man among multitudes of wicked men, women and children, admonishing his fellow citizens to get right with God and to stop their evil ways. But the people would not give heed and their wickedness so grieved God that He unleashed a gigantic flood that would cover the whole earth and rid it of evil.

God told Noah how to build the huge boat that would save him and his family. Having been given instruction for the ship design, Noah was instructed upon its completion to take on board his wife, three sons and their wives, plus male and female of the various species.

God Himself closed the door when Noah's family and the animals were safely on board. When they emerged from the ark many months later, Noah immediately fell on his knees in gratefulness to God for keeping them safe. He hurried to make preparation to build an altar and there he sacrificed several animals in a burnt offering of thanksgiving.

Generations and centuries went by, and Noah's descendants strived to keep alive the story of their forefather—the one so important that the God of this earth made special arrangements to save his life when all others perished. They told and retold the story of him safely navigating a huge boat through the waters of a flood that ravaged every other creature and every blade of grass.

Unfortunately, Noah's descendants soon forgot

that God had been good to their ancestor because, and only because, of his righteousness. Otherwise he and his family would have perished like everyone else. They began to build Noah up as some great hero who had outwitted God and saved himself. They minimized his righteous walk before God and instead idolized him as a man who had safely navigated the waters of a great flood; a man who had successfully contended with God and brought his family to safety when God planned evil upon him and the whole world.

Intentionally or unintentionally, a false religion was born. The fact that God Himself gave Noah the plan for safekeeping because of his righteousness was passed over as his descendants' minds darkened. They gave credit to Noah as having saved himself and sevens *by craftiness* when God sent the great deluge. Soon a belief evolved that passing safely through the waters was a symbolic way to gain God's favor and go to heaven. Their false belief caused a breach between man and God.

The myths surrounding Noah's prowess expanded. One example of the retelling of the Noah event is the early *Gilgamesh epic* studied worldwide in most college literature classes. On Tablet XI, it relates a flood story similar to Noah's in the Babylonian traditions. In it, Utnapishtim plays the part of Noah and, like Noah, he survives cosmic destruction by heeding divine orders to build an ark.[6]

In correlation with this falsification, another phenomena occurred that taken together, would further remove a relationship with God from men's minds.

The Bible includes the story in abbreviated form and it's almost too much for contemporary man to handle—though many stories and motion pictures try to wrap our minds around it so as to make sense of it.

> Now it came to pass, when men began to multiply on the face of the earth, and daughters were born to them, that the sons of God saw the daughters of men, that they were beautiful; and they took wives for themselves of all whom they chose....There were giants on the earth in those days, and also afterward, when the sons of God came in to the daughters of men and they bore children to them. Those were the mighty men who were of old, men of renown.
>
> —Genesis 6:1-4

The myths about Noah became intertwined with mankind's fascination with the fathering of these half angelic/half human beings. The offspring of these supernatural beings would be giants, men of renown, including Goliath the giant who was killed by the shepherd boy David. Four sons of one giant are mentioned as being killed by David's mighty men. Two of their names were Ishbi-Benob and Saph, (II Sam. 21:16; II Sam. 21:18).

People were curious about these facts and many myths would grow in the imaginations of men. The Greek classics by such poets as Homer are tales written about the deeds and misdeeds of these angelic beings, with a fictitious domicile assigned them on

Mt. Olympus. Out of these imaginings came stories of mythological exploits that account for the god/goddesses of Greek and Roman mythology as well as Hinduism, the mystery religions, sun worship and certain aspects found in Mormonism (LDS) as well.

The names of their deities multiplied because of the language confusion at the Tower of Babel and include such names as Isis, Artemis, Astarte, Aphrodite, Asheroth, Athena, Diana, etc. for the 'goddesses' as well a variety of names given to their sons/cohorts, including the various Baals and one in particular named Tammuz.

The New Testament continues the story of the fallen angels. We are told that God chained the angelic beings who conjoined with earth women and fathered the giants, in darkness under the earth. These fallen angels are referred to as the angels 'who left their first estate.'

There is no indication that all of the fallen angels who followed Satan in his rebellion joined in this activity but those that did remain God's prisoners. They are being held in darkness until Judgment Day where they will, no doubt, receive harsh judgment for starting the false religions that spread worldwide, leading multitudes away from redemption and a relationship with the true God:

> For if God did not spare the angels who sinned, but cast them down to hell and delivered them into chains of darkness, to be reserved for judgment...."
>
> —2 Peter 2:4-6

> And the angels who did not keep their proper domain, but left their own abode, He has reserved in everlasting chains under darkness for the judgment of the great day...."
>
> —Jude 6, 7

The Bible warns against fallen angelic beings who bring false religions. It says, "But even if we, or an angel from heaven, preach any other gospel to you than what we have preached to you, let him be accursed."[7] Unfortunately, there are two religions today that were given at different times by fallen angels to two illiterate men, Mohammed and Joseph Smith, Jr.

In 610 A.D., Mohammed met with an angel in a cave and was given 'a holy book' and told to start the Islam religion. Its purpose was to displace Christianity.[8] In 1823, the Mormon church (LDS) was started by another angel, Moroni, in a cave. Joseph Smith, Jr. said he, too, was told to start Mormonism in order to displace Christianity.[9]

If one hesitates to accept angelic interference in religion, consider, for example, the similarities found in these two religions, Islam and the Mormon (LDS) church, which seem more than mere coincidence. This would be expected in coming from the same source. (See Endnote[10].)

While stories of beings in the atmosphere seem ridiculously farfetched in today's realistic way of thinking, we can nonetheless see traces of how these belief systems emerged to become the mystery religions of Greece, Rome, Asia, and beyond. Even today we see women flurrying around the concept of "Sophia," first at the "RE-imagining" conferences and, more recently, in small groups within several of the churches that sponsored these conferences.

Most members in the infant baptism churches are not aware that a similar belief system is at the root of many pagan religions—the belief that 'baptism saves'—and which emerged as a result of the misinterpretation of the Noah and the ark story.[11]

If we could not see that there really were religions with mythological gods and goddesses in such religions as sun worship, Hinduism and the mystery religions, our western mindset would likely just dismiss all this as silliness. But—though unusual—these are the events that can be traced back to most of the false religions currently in the world today.[12]

All this 'goddess stuff' has brought great distrust to the worship of the one true God, especially among intellectuals. And who can blame them for embracing philosophy—a study of what man thinks about these things—as they attempt to understand God and their beginnings? But by using secondary sources instead of the Bible which is a primary source and has writings that go back in history for thousands of years with scores of impeccable authors inspired by God, they only deepen their unbelief.

A respected book to consult regarding the false god/goddess intrusion into Christianity through the Noahic myth is *The Two Babylons*, a book by the Rev. Alexander Hislop. His research authenticates much of the history of the god/goddess beliefs that are known collectively as the Mystery Religions and is foundational to much of the following information:

Hislop says that in India, land of a million gods, the main "god" is known by the name Vishnu, meaning "the Preserver." Vishnu's story is similar to Noah's in that he is credited with being supernaturally preserved along with a single righteous family when great worldwide flooding occurred, drowning the rest of the world. In Sanskrit, Vishnu means Noah. In Chaldean, the word for Noah is similar: "Ish-nuh" means "Man of rest."[13]

When the Adamic race spread worldwide after their failed attempt to build the Tower of Babel,[14] the masses having been dispersed when God divided them into people groups through the use of various languages,[15] the name of their deities would also mutate slightly.[16] Yet goddess worship had been established by the residents of Babel and would remain shockingly similar.[17]

The names of the original priest and priestess at the tower of Babel were Nimrod and Semiramas. According to books on ancient Greek and Roman religions, when Nimrod died, his widow Semiramas claimed that a son, Tammuz, was conceived by a sunbeam after her husband's death. She declared that her husband was now a sun god in heaven. This, according to her, made her baby son a sun god and she, herself, became queen of heaven *and mother of God!*[18]

This has resulted in a baby sun god and "queen of heaven" worship in religions around the world. Examples are Fortuna and Jupiter; Isis and Horus[19] and, of course, it has infiltrated the Roman Catholic Church in the form of Madonna and son.[20] Most Christians unwittingly enter into observances with the false gods and goddesses of mythology when they celebrate the birthday of Jesus on December 25th,

In the pagan world, long before the Roman Catholic church claimed December 25th as the birthday of Jesus, it was celebrated worldwide as the birthday of the sun god which included Zeus, Tammuz, Ra and Mithra (which later entered Rome and was Rome's official state religion at the time of Constantine). In fact, when Rome conquered Jerusalem, they hung Jewish patriots on the cross of Mithra on December 25th as a sacrifice to the sun god.[21]

Ever wonder why, during Lent, one mourns forty days before Jesus' death on the cross? This practice, too, can be traced back to the goddess religions. Supposedly, Tammuz, a fertility god, was gored by a wild boar and died. He descended into the netherworld. His mother searched for him (some versions say it was his consort, Ishtar). She finally found him but with his reproductive organ missing. She mourns for forty days as she searches the netherworld for the lost organ. Earth women, too, mourn because all fertility has ceased.

On the fortieth day, the lost is found and the two ascend back upon earth amidst immoral revelry at a festival which we today call Easter.[22] Another 'Easter' myth has Ishtar falling to earth in a giant egg, hence today's celebrations of bunnies and eggs.

The book of Ezekiel tells of God's anger that Jewish women were also taking part in this festival.[23]

> So He brought me to the door of the north gate of the Lord's house; and to my dismay, women were sitting there weeping for Tammuz...and they were worshiping the sun toward the east.
>
> —Ezekiel 8:14-16

Another belief found in today's Christianity that also has its roots in paganism is the belief that one is saved in the waters of baptism. The belief that 'baptism saves' originated with the occultic Chaldeans—the land of idolatry which Abraham, father of our faith, was told to leave. The Chaldeans initiated sun worship where, if one desired to become a follower of the sun god, he was required to first submit to a violently rigorous baptism.[24] If he survived the ordeal, he was promised "regeneration" and forgiveness of all past sins.[25]

The ancestors of today's Scandinavians also believed that 'baptism saves.' Worshipers of the pagan god Odin, they practiced a baptism of infants and believed that "the natural guilt and corruption of new-born children"[26] was washed away in a baptism of infants. Although it took their rulers 150-200 years to force Scandinavians to a half-hearted acceptance of Catholicism and later to Lutheranism—one thing remained stable—their practice of infant baptism. Any of their religions was only a stone's throw from what they had already been doing.[27]

Meanwhile in Mexico, half a world away, the practice of infant baptism with its corresponding practice of baptismal regeneration was also taking place. When the explorer Cortez discovered the Aztecs, he was surprised to find them baptizing babies, too. It was strikingly similar to what was already being performed by Roman Catholic missionaries.[28] There, too, the god Odin was being worshiped, as well as the queen of heaven who is also worshiped among the Chaldeans, Persians and in the Canaanite religions.[29]

A Mexican[30] myth with Wodan (interchangeably called Odin) being a grandson of Noah who was saved on a raft when most of humanity perished in a great flood."[31] He is presented as one who cooperated in the construction of a great building undertaken by men to reach the skies.[32] Once more, we find evidence of the Noah story and its accompanying belief in baptismal regeneration.

Sooner or later someone will think to ask where a belief in baptizing babies comes from if "baptismal regeneration" through infant baptism is not a biblical principle. The scholar in the Roman and Greek mythological classics might immediately recognize the origins of this Roman Catholic doctrine of *"Limbo"* as originally coming from a poem titled *Aenid* that was written by Virgil a Roman poet.[33]

In *Aenid* the story is told of a man named *Aeneas* who descends into the hot, sulphuric regions of hell and finds the souls of tormented infants. It tells of innocent babes whom Death has cruelly snatched from their mother's bosom before they could be given the "rites" of the church—that is, infant baptism:

> Before the gates the cries of babes new-

born, whom fate had from their tender mothers torn, assault his ears.[34]

The epic goes on to speak of the horror of these 'wretched babes' who have been eternally excluded from paradise (called the *Elysian Fields*) because their parents neglected to submit them to a ritual of infant baptism. Now, so the poem goes, they are to forever lay in torment alongside suicides who "prodigally threw their souls away." [35]

The Roman Catholic church adopted this myth as doctrine for their church (it is not found in the Bible) and it, understandably, put great fear into the soft hearts of parents who feared for their little ones. As a result, they hurried their offspring off to the Roman church which, they were taught, had the authority to properly minister the rites of baptism so their little son or daughter did not end up in hell's fire.

The Roman Catholic church has now changed their mind about this doctrine they called being in "Limbo." According to Pope Benedict XVI, their church offices were having to deal with too many calls having to do with the eternal destination of aborted babies so they decided to do away with that belief altogether.

According to an article in the *Minneapolis Star Tribune*, on December 5, 2005, the Roman Catholic church issued a report to prepare the hearts of its adherents around the world that a change was coming regarding the doctrine of Limbo. Then, on January 10, 2006, Pope Benedict XVI called a press conference to do the actual business of taking apart the doctrine of Limbo. He told the press that Limbo had always been "only a hypothesis" anyway.[36]

The next question for concerned parents then would be what *does happen* when a baby dies before he is old enough to decide for himself things of an eternal matter? Believers need not fear; God has it all well in hand:

> For the unbelieving husband is sanctified by the wife, and the unbelieving wife is sanctified by the husband; otherwise your children would be unclean, but now they are holy."

—I Corinthians 7:14

When one reads the above verse, it is interesting to note that God did not need man to come up with a ritual to "save" believers' babies. The root of God's declaration of our offspring as being 'holy' is the same as is used for God's Holy Spirit!

> Strong's Exhaustive Concordance of Bible Words: #40; Greek: *hagios.* Means Physically pure; morally blameless or religious; consecrated; most holy; saints." Also see No. 53; No. 2282.

So God apparently sees our little ones as pure of heart and not in need of infant baptism to exorcise a devil in them because the same word, *hagios,* as is used in the Bible to refer to a Christian's baby, is also used to refer to the Holy Spirit!

Not only that, the Bible states that if one becomes evil, his name is *blotted out of* the Book of Life. This suggests that all human beings are originally in the

Book of Life. Their name is removed when they refuse God's offer of redemption.

So it is their own choices that remove their name from the Book of Life—baby baptism has nothing to do with it!

---

[1] www.noahsark-naxuan.com/1.htm
[2] KJV Amplified Holy Bible-Parallel Bible. 10
[3] Ibid.
[4] Genesis 6-8
[5] II Peter 2:5
[6] "Noah" Encyclopaedia Britannica *online:*
www.search.eb.com/bol/topic?eu=57401&sctn=1[accessed 18 September 2001]
[7] Galatians 1:8
[8] www.allaboutreligion.org/Origin-Of-Islam.htm
[9] www.exmormon.org/tract2.htm
[10] www.bible.ca/islam/islamic-mormonism-similarities.htm www.bible.ca/islam/islamic-mormonism-similarities.htm
findarticles.com/p/articles/mi_qn4188/is_20110313/ai_n57069290/
www.uvu.edu/religiousstudies/mormonismandislam/ ;
Some similarities between the two religions whose founders say they were given them by an angel are that both started by fallen angels, both men claimed to be illiterate; both men visited by angelic beings in a cave; both men given religious books that were not the Bible; both men told their new religion would replace Old Testament Judaism and New Testament Christianity; both told that Jesus was not God; both told Jesus was a prophet but not God; Polygamy was to be a part of both; both were to be re-

warded after death with multiple sexual partners; both worship Allah (Islam openly; Mormons in the high echelons of their religion); both murdered 'infidels' on 9/ll. (Mormons in the Mountain Meadow Massacre and Muslims in New York City); both erected monuments to themselves or attempted to do so (Mormon temple in Nauvoo, IL); Muslims attempted same at Ground Zero (New York City).

[11] See *The Secret About Infant Baptism That Everyone's Missing. Amazon.com*

[12] Anderson, Sir Norman. *Christianity and World Religions*. Leicester, England: InterVarsity Press, 1984, 65.

[13] Ibid. 59 (Also Wilson's India Three Thousand Years Ago)

[14] Genesis 11:1-10

[15] Genesis 10, 11

[16] Rives, Richard M. Too Long in the Sun. (Partakers Publications, Charlotte, NC. 1997, 51-76; The Zondervan Pictorial Encyclopedia of the Bible, Vol. 3, 334.

[17] Hislop, A. *The Two Babylons*. Neptune, NJ: Loizeaux Brothers, 1916, 132; Bonnefay. *246;* Davies. 69.

[18] Ibid.

[19] Hislop, A. *The Two Babylons*. Neptune, NJ: Loizeaux Brothers, 1916; 140. (Also Pompeii, vol. ii. P.150)

[20] Hunt, D. *A Woman Rides the Beast*. Eugene, OR: Harvest House Publishers, 1994, 430. (also Wagner, 31.) Ezekiel 8:14; Jeremiah 7:18.

[21] Ruud, 61-62.

[22] *The Zondervan Pictorial Encyclopedia of The Bible*, Vol.3, 334. Ruud, 65-66.

[23] Ezekiel 8:14

[24] Bonnefay. 246; Davies. 69.

[25] Hislop. 132; (Also Eliase Comment. In 8. Greg. Naz., Orat. Iv.' Gredorii Nazanzine Opera, p.245)

[26] Ibid. *(Also Mallet on Anglo-Saxon Baptism, Antiquities, vol.i., p.335)*
[27] Ibid.
[28] Ibid. *(Humboldt's Mexican Researches, Vol.i., pp.185)*
[29] Ibid. *(Prescott's Mexico, Vol.iii. pp.339-340.)*
[30] *According to the ancient traditions collected by Bishop Francis Nunez de la Vega*
[31] Whyte. 32-33
[32] Ibid. *133. (Humboldt's Researches, Vol.I. p.320).*
[33] Hislop, 239. (Aeneid, Book vi.ll. 576-578, Dryden.—In Original, ll. 427-429)
[34] Aeneid, Book vi.ll. 576-578, Dryden.—In Original, ll. 427-429.
[35] Virgil, Book vi 586-589, Dryden's Translation. – Original, ll. 434-436.
[36] Kevin Horragan, "The Afterlife: Limbo Rocked," Knight-Ridder News Service, January 10, 2006.

PART II

THE MISSING FACTOR

13
TIME WARP

Pagan gods and goddesses are nothing new. The Bible, however, gives insight into why there are false religions in the world with some showing up in history centuries before Christianity.

This is a fact that has caused men and women who consider themselves intellectuals no end of problems. They seek to study philosophy and the religions of the world to figure out which is the right religion and which one will get them to heaven—or even if there is a God.

Most know that it is not only the infant baptism churches that teach that 'baptism saves,' but that Hinduism teaches this, the Mormon/LDS church teaches it, the Mystery Religions teach it as does Sun Worship. Not only that, Hinduism and the Mormon/LDS church even teaches that you can 'save' dead people by baptizing them in water.

In the Christian church, the doctrine of infant baptism has many people fooled which is the reason I began researching the origins of infant baptism in the first place. Because I already knew from spending a year researching, among other things, the doctrine of baptism—that there is no example given in the Bible of an infant baptism. (See *The Question about Infant Baptism: Does Baptism Save?*)

There have been centuries of foxhole conversions but that is not what they are after. They want a belief system that can stand the rigors of investigation—

one whose facts they can believe in and count on in times of trouble and times of happiness—one where concrete facts are spelled out that lead to faith—genuine faith.

Today there are many religions that have as their central figure a mother and son. Many of these religions predate Christianity, sometimes by thousands of years but still have some similarities such as blood sacrifice, miraculous happenings; even rituals of water baptism and stories of a resurrection—although there were no witnesses.

To understand how so many false world religions got started, one must go back to verses given in the Bible regarding how God let His plan of redemption be known before the foundations of the world ever were put in place. This allowed Satan the opportunity to develop a counterfeit religion and put it in place before it was timing for His plan of redemption to be revealed—and we wonder why? What was God's purpose for doing this? Was it to force Satan's hand and get him to show clearly his hand of deception—or were there other reasons?

> "He indeed was foreordained before the foundation of the world, but was manifest in these last times for you."
> —I Peter 1:20

> "… the Lamb slain from the foundation of the world."
> —Revelation 13:8

It is odd that the above verses have been almost completely ignored or at least they have not quoted as insight as to why there are so many religions—some coming centuries before Christianity and causing us mankind to question whether Jesus Christ really is the Son of God and if His death on the cross really has the power to set them free from their past.

Yet it is a truth clearly put forth in the Bible that God's plan of redemption was known—perhaps eons ahead of time—even before the foundations of the world were laid. More than three hundred prophecies heralded this fact. This alerted all angelic forces—*good and evil*—to His plans ahead of time.

This is of interest to us because many have studied ancient mythology and are cognizant of the details of the world religions on earth today. They have taken note that Christianity was not the earliest religion in the world (nor was Old Testament Judaism, for that matter). They wonder how that could be if God truly is who He says He is?

In the Book of Genesis, first chapter of the Bible, a story of Creation begins to unwind and in it we are warned against deception. In that idyllic first story, God forms a man and calls him Adam and then forms a wife for him.

Satan, in the form of a serpent, hurries to Eve's side, feigning innocence of God's plan. Seductively he croons, "Has God *really said* you shall not eat of every tree of the garden?" And then he said, "surely you will not die *and it will make you wise.*"

Eve ate of the Tree of the Knowledge of Good and Evil and gave to Adam and he did east. So deception began in the Garden of Eden! Satan had tricked Eve into eating the forbidden fruit and the damage was done. Man's knowledge of evil has caused him pain every day of his life since then.

God did not mince words when He told Satan he would be cursed because of his deception of Eve and He added: "The woman's son will crush thy head and you will bruise His heel."

Satan had brought a curse down upon his own head. He must have wondered if he could somehow avert that curse and started his own counterfeit religion. If so, it served two purposes. It deflected worship from God and continued his deception upon mankind.

A woman's son would crush his head? Could he possibly crush the son *before that happened?* In today's false religions, God the Father is almost overlooked. Man is put in that position and God is left a very weak player; He is set aside while *a woman and her baby son* become centerpiece deities; she becoming 'queen of heaven' and 'mother of God.'

This is true in sun worship; this is true in the papal systems of Europe with "Our Lady," Madonna and son. It was also true in Egypt with Isis and Osiris;[1] in India, Isi and Iswarea;[2] and in Asia with Cybele and Deoius. In pagan Rome, it was Fortuna and Jupiter, the boy (and later as Mithra the sun god).[3]

This counterfeit combination of mother and son can also be found in Greece, Tibet, China, and Japan. In these mother/son religions, the mother is known as the "Queen of Heaven" and 'Mother of God" as well as the "Great Mother Goddess. (The great mother goddess is seen today with Wiccans and Sophia.)

As noted earlier, the Bible records Satan's next actions. Satan did not want a pure 'seed' to be found through whom God could send a Redeemer. In order to keep that from happening after he had corrupted the human race, he needed to destroy God's plan for a holy 'Seed' to come through mankind.[4]

The Bible states in its minimalist way what transpired next. The sons of God (What were they? Who were they? Were they fallen angelic beings? Were they a different variety of being?) slunk into the abode of the daughters of men where they produced unusual offspring that Satan would use in his plan. Even King David had a battle with one of the offspring of the 'sons of God' when he confronted Goliath on the battlefield as found in the Old Testament.[5]

Sound farfetched? The Bible admits that 'mighty' men were born of these unions. Mythology tells tall tales of the deeds (no doubt magnified) of these beings but it gave fodder that Satan could use to put false religion in place with supposed 'gods and goddesses.' The adversary of our souls had plenty of time to counterfeit a religion using the details God had let be known ahead of time. As a result, false religion manifested many years before God's predetermined time for the redemption of mankind to take place.

Because God's plan—and possibly even the deed—took place in the heavenlies before the foundation of the world, the concept of *time warp* and the possibility that Jesus was physically crucified before the foundations of the world cannot be ruled out. It might have seemed impossible even a few decades ago. But now with the concept of *time warp* almost universally understood—at least in part—the possibility that Jesus could have been crucified before the world began causes hardly a blink of the eye.

But in being willing to acknowledge the concept of time warp, one must also accept the fact that if Jesus was crucified eons before the deed was manifested in real time two thousand years ago—if that's what happened—Satan had plenty of time to put a counterfeit religion in place (and steal certain details from God's plan) before the appointed time for Christ to come to earth to die on the cross.

Another detail that God gave beforehand was that a virgin would bear a son.[6] There it was! The fact that Satan apparently keyed in on was that a virgin would bear a son. As revealed in the Garden of Eden, it was this Son who would crush Satan's head.

But again—a virgin bearing a son? Not a hard concept for contemporary man, what with the newspapers full of stories of surrogate motherhood, *in vitro* fertilization and cloning. But even if God's plan for the Virgin Mary giving birth to His Son was completely different than any of these, modern man has little difficulty wrapping his mind around even that possibility.

Now all that is left for the crime to be solved is to find 'the smoking gun'—the false religion originated by Satan at the Tower of Babel for the purpose of deceiving mankind!

[1] *Two Babylons* by Alexander Hislop, 20. (Also *Osiris,* as the child called most frequently Horus. Bunsen, vol. i. p.438, compared with pp. 433, 434.)

[2] Ibid. (Kennedy's *Hindoo Mythology, p. 49. Though Iswara is the husband of Isi, he is also represented as an infant at her breast. Ibid. p.338, Note.)*

[3] Ibid. (*Cicero's works, De Divinatione*, lib. H. cap. 41, vol. iii, p. 77.)

[4] Genesis 6:4; Jude 6,7

[5] I Samuel 17

[6] Isaiah 7:14

14
SUN WORSHIP – THE SMOKING GUN

We do not need to look any further to find the smoking gun than the mother/son religions of the world. Now Jesus' humble mum has been added to the list by the Roman Catholic church.

A single template for these religions has been used—same goddess, same baby, same belief that 'baptism saves.' Only the names of the 'goddess' and her 'son' change. Some examples are Cybele, Astarte, Asheroth, Isis, Ishtar, Beltis and others—each has been known in their own nation or area as "queen of heaven," "mother of god" or "my lady." Each has a baby boy: Tammuz, Baal, Nin, etc., etc.

The goddess religions as devised by Satan would use a false water baptism (the belief that baptism saves) to deceive mankind. This can be seen in the 1.2 billion member Roman Catholic church and in the almost half a billion member Protestant churches—many of which also teach an infant baptism.

Many other false world religions also have a belief that 'baptism saves.' Examples are Hinduism and Mormonism (the LDS movement) with both presumptuously believing they can even baptize the dead, bringing them out of hell into heaven with a manmade ceremony.

Well-known evangelist of the nineteenth century, Charles Spurgeon, attempted to warn the Christian church of the deception found in infant baptism. He pointed out that baptism *does not save* and declared it to be the worst of all heresies. He said it was put in place to deceive those seeking God.

> Of all lies which have dragged millions down to hell, I look upon this [baptismal regeneration] as being one of the most atrocious. Baptismal regeneration is an error that has damned millions of souls.[1]

Indeed, the belief that one can be regenerated by being baptized in water is a primitive, pagan belief having to do with water's regenerative properties. Seeing the greening of vegetation after a rain or a flood led ancient man to worship demonic spiritual beings known as *vegetation* or *fertility* gods and goddesses—including today's popular Isis and Osiris children's cartoons:

> ...during the Roman period, with the clear Egyptianization of the Isiac (Isis) religion and the popularity of the Isiac Mysteries and initiation that promised the initiate life in the afterworld, there was a renewed interest in Osiris. Osiris was associated with the holy water of the Nile, a symbol of fertility and resurrection, which played a great part in the ritual of the Isiac temples of the

Roman Empire."[2]

A false twist of the Noah and the flood story has permeated Greek and Roman mythological literature. Written by well known authors such as Homer, Euripides, and Sophocles, they are taught in both our high schools and colleges.[3] As the percentage of Gentiles increased in the Christian church and the number of Jews declined after the fall of Jerusalem in 70 A.D., the clear distinction between Christianity and the mystery religions became clouded. The Jews were no longer a part of the church so weren't there to watch and keep sun worship at bay.

The sun god was the predominant god worshiped by both the emperor and his soldiers and was the official state religion in Rome all during the Emperor Constantine's reign. It had entered Roman civilization between 88-63 B.C. Shrines especially abounded in Germany; but after World War II, the bombing unearthed a statue of the sun god near London.[4]

The Old Testament Jews had been deceived by sun worship. In the Book of Ezekiel, the Jewish women were worshiping the sun god, Tammuz:

> "So He brought me to the door of the north gate of the Lord's house; and to my dismay, women were sitting there weeping for Tammuz."
> —Ezekiel 8:14

Eight verses later, there is further detail on the activities of the Jews as they stand worshiping the sun:

> "So He brought me into the inner court of the Lord's house; and there, at the door of the temple of the Lord, between the porch and the altar, were about twenty-five men with their backs toward the temple of the Lord and their faces toward the east, and they were worshiping the sun toward the east."
> —Ezekiel 8:16

But that's not all! Two chapters later, God's presence leaves Israel because of the false worship that is taking place in the Jerusalem temple:

> "Then the glory of the Lord departed from the threshold of the temple and stood over the cherubim. And the cherubim lifted their wings and mounted up from the earth in my sight...."
> —Ezekiel 10:18-19

As the percentage of Gentiles increased in the Christian church and the number of Jews declined after the fall of Jerusalem in 70 A.D., the clear distinction between Christianity and the Mystery Religions became clouded. The Jews were no longer a part of the church so weren't there to watch and keep sun worship at bay. Their ancestors had been exposed to sun worship while in exile in Babylon and wanted nothing more to do with it.

Yet the weakening of the Christian church by the persecution of the pagan emperors caused the churches to be in disarray as their buildings were destroyed, their Scriptures burned, their pastors im-

SUN WORSHIP – THE SMOKING GUN

prisoned and killed, leaving the new Gentile converts to flounder. Sun worship began to regain some of its prior strength and become a rival to the early Church.

Rome's citizens were also sun worshipers plus they added on any number of other religions—as many as they could afford. They believed it was necessary to worship the many gods and goddesses found in the writings of their culture in order to have things "go well" in their lives.

The Romans looked up into the sky and concluded that the sun god was of a "higher power" than evil and darkness. So, although emperors were often worshiped by their citizens, they themselves aligned themselves with "power" by making the sun god their god of choice. Sun worshipers were believers in *"baptismal regeneration."*

Those who worshiped the sun god underwent elaborate water ceremonies that promised to initiate its adherents, through a series of stages, into immortality and heaven. The water for these baptismal rites was supplied through a system of aqueducts.

The center of this area reserved for performance of a blood ritual. A bull was slain and the priests, covered with the hot blood of the freshly-slain bull would come forth before the congregation, "covered in the blood." If worshipers survived their violently rigorous water baptism, the religion promised them forgiveness and "resurrection" and "a crown of life."[5]

The early Church was especially concerned about the counterfeit provided in sun worship as it was the predominant god worshiped by both the emperor and his soldiers. It was the official state religion at the time of Constantine, having entered Roman civilization between 88-63 B.C. Shrines especially abounded in Germany but after the bombings of World War II, a statue of the sun god was even unearthed near London.[6]

Tertullian, respected early Church historian, complained that in its effort to pervert the truth, sun worship closely mimicked the "divine sacraments" found in Christianity—that of water baptism and promises of forgiveness given through the shed blood of a bull. Claims of a "resurrection" were also made.[7]

Water baptism as practiced in the New Testament began to change to become more like that of the mystery religions.[8] In the New Testament, baptism was done immediately after a new convert repented of his sins. It was then followed by receiving the gift of the Holy Spirit. This pattern was not to change until the Second Coming of Jesus and was given in every example in the New Testament.

> ...Repent, and let every one of you be baptized into the name of Jesus Christ for the remission of sin; and you will receive the gift of the Holy Spirit. The promise is to you and to your children and to all who are afar off, as many as the Lord our God will call.
>
> —Acts 2:38-39

Soon changes began to evolve that were similar to

the baptism ritual in sun worship; i.e., it began to be believed that one was actually 'saved' in the waters of baptism and this belief was eventually transferred into a *baptismal regeneration* ritual for infants.

Goddess worship is not a light amusement. It caused God to abandon the Jerusalem Temple and Israel was overrun with her enemies. The Jews were driven into exile in Babylon in 586 A.D. The original sun worship took place there at the Tower of Babel. Once in exile, the Jews saw firsthand the depths of degradation expected of those involved in sun worship and they turned back to the worship of Jehovah. For the past 2,500 years, they have not returned to the idolatrous worship of the sun god.

No longer welcome in Old Testament Judaism, worship of the sun god turned toward the Church—God's other people.

---

[1] Baptismal Regeneration the Great Pagan Idol by Rev. V. L. Peterson, 3.

[2] *Greek and Egyptian Mythologies* by Yves Bonnefoy. 246+

[3] en.wikipedia.org/wiki/Apollonian_and_Dionysian

[4] Christian History, Issue 37, "Worshiping Like Pagans." 16.

[5] Ibid.

[6] Christian History, Issue 37, "Worshiping Like Pagans." 16.

[7] Ibid.

[8] Acts 2:38, 39

15
SUN WORSHIP & THE CATHOLIC CHURCH

The Emperor Constantine was not the benefactor of the church as he is commonly portrayed. The fact that he was also serving as high priest of paganism is glossed over in books that sensationalize his reign and assistance of the Christian church. In truth, he was trying to coordinate the church and the pagan religions in his empire so as to produce a peaceful setting for his throne. It must be remembered that all before and all during the Emperor Constantine's reign that sun worship was the state religion.

He was popular with his Roman citizens including the Christians because he ordered all persecution *for all religions* to stop. So great had been the persecution *of Christians* during the prior reign of the previous emperor, Emperor Diocletian, that the church at Rome had nearly been gutted. Diocletian had ordered all Christian Scripture and literature burned, all pastors imprisoned, all churches destroyed and all laypeople forced to burn incenses to the emperor or suffer the consequences.

Once Diocletian had done his dirty work, he then abdicated the throne. This was in 305 A.D.

In 306 A.D., Constantine entered the throne at Rome. After all the cruel persecution, he became the darling who restored the church—at the same time—he would completely change the future Roman Catholic church! For the first time in Roman history, he ordered all religious persecution to stop. This favor was bestowed on Christian and pagan alike and he furthermore extended to his citizens the hitherto unheard of right to choose their own religion.

A future emperor, Theodosius, would be the one to make Christianity the state religion of Rome. This was in 378 A.D. Theodosius then went a step further and declared Church membership compulsory and outlawed all other religions that did not comply with the Roman church's practices—this included baptizing infants into the Roman church. This excluded all who refused to be baptized into the Roman church.

The Emperor Theodosius made the 'church' the new state religion and ordered all Roman citizens to become members. Unfortunately, this filled the churches to overflowing with unregenerate people, including the Vandals and the Goths. The result was a further assault on Christianity for the Roman Catholic church of Rome became filled with unregenerated, hardhearted people without faith, without repentance, and without a soft heart toward the things of God-and they were without faith in Jesus Christ.[1]

All they needed to do was be baptized in water to become a 'Christian'—the very method used in sun worship to recruit new members. Although Rome's new religion officially became the *Roman Catholic Church,* it was not actually a church as described in the Book of Acts but was a *syncretism* (with the definition syncretism being two or more religions melded into one new *and different* religion).

In the case of the Roman Catholic church, the syncretism was a combination of sun worship and Christianity. The names of the sun god would morph until it entered the Roman Empire as Mithra and from there, when the queen of heaven and mother of god entered the church as the Madonna, the name given her son was Jesus.

Other rituals and ceremonies and beliefs from sun worship soon followed. Some that are in the Roman Catholic church today are the following:

1. *December 25:* One well known tradition from sun worship that would be added to the Roman Catholic church was the December 25th date traditionally celebrated as the birthday of the sun god. In the Roman church, it would become a 'white-washed' celebration of Christ's birthday and this would spread to the Protestant church.[2]

2. *Easter:* Another observance was the licentious celebration of the spring equinox which, again, became a white-washed day to observe Jesus' resurrection.'[3] Today we recognize it by the name of Easter.

3. *Idolatry:* Although the Ten Commandments require that we do not make for ourselves any graven image or any image of anything in the heavens above or the earth beneath, the Roman Catholic church

has taken the graven images made by pagans of their deities and re-titled them with 'christianized' names. One example is the statue of Zeus which was re-titled and even later, remade, calling it St. Peter and giving it a place of honor in the Basilica.[4]

4. *Sunday:* The observance of *Deis Solis*—the Day of the Sun—had been substituted for the biblical Sabbath.[5] This first occurred under the reign of Constantine who even had coins made that gave reverence to the sun god.

5. *Mother of God and Queen of Heaven:* The Roman church has substituted pagan worship of the goddess Cybele (and other goddesses associated with sun worship) who was known as the "mother of god" and "queen of heaven" long before Catholics began to worship Mary mother of Jesus as the Madonna and also as the "mother of God" and "queen of heaven."[6]

6. *Prayers for the dead* did not originate with Catholicism, either. Other pagan religions did the same long before it was done in what would become the Roman *universal* church. Though thought to be strictly a Catholic observance;, they were first found in Egyptian idolatry,[7] and also practiced in ancient Greece[8] and in India.[9]

7. The Roman Catholic church has long in-

dulged in idol processions and relic worship that comes out of paganism.[10] This is also true of their habit of crowning of images of the mother-and-child by using a sunburst halo. These halos of light often are shown in medieval portraits as surrounding the heads of Mary, Jesus and even stepfather, Joseph. Sunburst halos come straight out of sun worship![11]

8. *Rosaries*, a way of praying using chains and beads is still in this day and age a practice of many pious Catholics who have never thought to research its origins. In truth, however, praying by use of a form of the rosary is almost universally found in such pagan religions as the Hindu Brahmins, Tibetans, Buddhists, the ancient Mexicans and others.[12]

9. *Purgatory*, the belief that after centuries of torment one can be purified and make atonement for their sin thus giving them a second chance of gaining heaven after death is also of pagan origin. It is found in Greek and Roman mythology.[13] This gives them a false hope for the Bible says this decision to repent and follow Christ must be made in this life, in the here and now for the Bible says "It is given unto men once to die, and then the judgment."

10. *Limbo:* Pope Benedict XVI debunked

'limbo' in 2006 when he said the Roman Catholic church never really believed in it anyway – it was just a hypothesis.

11. *Praying to Mary:* This comes out of sun worship. She is just one more name in a long line of names such as Ishtar, Isis, Asharoth, Astarte, Venus, etc. who mythology claimed as mothers of the 'sun' god.

12. *Infant Baptism*: Infant baptism is the most serious of all major changes that were brought into the Roman Catholic church. This was because it would steal the born again experience of repentance and faith in the blood Jesus shed on the cross. By believing that 'baptism saves,' pious church members would lose their salvation.

As the percentage of Gentiles left the pagan religions that taught these things and entered the Christian church increased and the number of Jews declined after the fall of Jerusalem in 70 A.D., the clear distinction between Christianity and sun worship became clouded.

The early Church was especially concerned about the counterfeit provided in sun worship.[14] Tertullian, respected early Church historian, complained that in its effort to pervert the truth, sun worship closely mimicked the "divine sacraments" found in Christianity—that of water baptism and promises of forgiveness albeit through the shed blood of a bull. Claims of a "resurrection" were also made.[15]

[1] www.en.wikipedia.org/wiki/Collections_of_ancient_canons#Papal_decretals

[2] Rives, Richard M. *Too Long in the Sun.* (Partakers Publications, Charlotte, NC. 1997. 62.
www.toolong.com/christmas.htm

[3] www.lasttrumpetministries.org/tracts/tract1.html

[4] www.joshua-of-nazareth.org/abomination-of-desolation.html

[5] www.biblesabbath.org/index.php?pr=Catholic_and_Protestant_Confessions

[6] www.crossroad.to/articles2/2002/carl-teichrib/5isis.htm

[7] Hislop. 168. [also Dryden's *Virgil,,* Book vi. ll. 995-1012, vol. ii. p.536; in original, ll.730-747.]

[8] Ibid. [also *Dorians,* vol. *ii.* P. 405.]

[9] Ibid. [also *Asiatic Researches,* vol. *vii.* pp.239, 240.]

[10] www.themeaningofislam.org/beliefs/death/prayers_for_the_deceased.html www.urbandharma.org/kusala/dad.html

[11] www.masters-table.org/pagan/sun2.htm

[12] Ibid. [also Humboldt, vol.ii. p. 20.]

[13] www.mtc.org/purgtory.html

[14] Christian History, Issue 37, "Worshiping Like Pagans." 16.

[15] Ibid.

16
CHRISTMAS, EASTER AND WHAT?

The origins of the goddess religions with their mother/son template have played a huge part in the corruption found in today's churches.

Even Christmas, that bastion of relatives gathered under one roof, gifts under a green tree loaded with silver and gold ornaments, a Yule log brought in from the great outdoors and children's wide-eyed expectation of Christmas morning wealth; has felt its taint.

We have been told that Christmas—December 25th—is a day specifically set aside for celebrating Jesus' birthday. Most know this is not the actual birthdate of Christ but indulge the calendar anyway, believing it is as good a day as any to put on display our feelings of good will toward man and also an opportunity to put a harmless baby Jesus on public display.

Good feelings aside, however, the December 25th date chosen for this celebration, goes back to a sinister occasion noted in the book of Ezekiel where, we are told of the worship of a "god" named Tammuz. It reads.

> The angel brought me to the gate of the house of the Lord and I beheld—women weeping for Tammuz. (Ezekiel 8:14)

The pagan god, Tammuz, one of the names for the sun god, is the one with the original December 25th birthday! We are taken back in time to the events found from reading Genesis 10 and 11. Much more than an ancient story, it is still affecting us today. The Bible states that Nimrod (a descendant of Noah) built a city on the plains of Shinar. On this site, the infamous Tower of Babel was built—called Babel today because it was there that God confused the language of the people so that they sounded like "babblers" to each other. They had been prematurely attempting to collaborate by forming a 'one world' government and religion in order to "do all they planned." It was here that false religion got its start.

The Bible speaks of a man named Nimrod as an evil man who 'hunted" down the souls of men. Jewish tradition credits Shem, Noah's oldest son, with slaying Nimrod in righteous indignation because of his deception of mankind. His body parts were scattered throughout the land of Shinar, thus did he hope to put an end to the false worship of Nimrod.[1]

Instead, Nimrod's followers erected a huge obelisk made to symbolize Nimrod's uncircumcised reproductive organ. Similar obelisks are seen worldwide today in Rome, London, Heliopolis (Egypt), Paris, the Washington monument in D.C., and New York City. The Bible refers to them as "the image of jealousy."

> "...and brought me in visions of God to Jerusalem, to the door of the north gate of the in-

ner court, where the seat of the image of jealousy was, which provokes to jealousy." (Ezekiel 8:3)

After Nimrod's death, his widow, Semiramus (called by various names because of the confusion of languages) became pregnant. She, according to books such as *Roman-Greek Mythology* by Yves Bonnefay, insisted she had become pregnant by a sunbeam. She secured her position as ruler by claiming she had conceived by her husband who was now sun god and resided in heaven. On the ancient Babylonian calendar, Winter Solstice fell on December 25th—which day they claim that Nimrod, sun god, was reborn as Tammuz.'[2]

The ancient Jews were familiar with this explanation. It was one of the reasons they were aghast when they saw some of the Christian churches taking on the trappings of sun worship. According to *The Pagan-Christian Connection Exposed*,[3] the Jews had become involved in sun worship when they were captives in Egypt. There they worshiped Ra, the Egyptian sun god, for more than four hundred years.

According to tradition (and similar to the beliefs that surrounded Tammuz as sun god), Ra was born on December 25th. In 168 B.C., the Syrian/Greek General Antiochus Epiphanes and his army occupied Jerusalem. On December 25th, Antiochus desecrated the temple by setting up a statue of Zeus on December 25th to celebrate his birthday and proclaiming Zeus god.

> So He brought me into the inner court of the Lord's house; and there, at the door of the temple of the Lord, between the porch and the altar, were about twenty-five men with their backs toward the temple of the Lord and their faces toward the east, and they were worshiping the sun toward the east. (Ezekiel 8:16)

It was not unusual for Roman armies to embrace the gods of the foreign lands they conquered. When Rome conquered Persia, their army began worshiping the Persian sun god, Mithra—a version of the Babylonian sun god, Tammuz. The symbol for both was a "T" or "cross," using the Greek letter, "tau," as a symbol of Tammuz' worshipers. When Rome conquered Jerusalem, they hung Jews on the cross of Mithra on December 25th—as a way of celebrating Mithra's birthday.

In the Book of Ruth, Elimelech left Bethlehem with his wife and two sons to journey into the land of Moab. Their sons eventually married local girls including Ruth who would become an ancestor of both King David and Jesus. Eventually, Elimelech and his two sons died, leaving his wife Naomi and her two daughters-in-law widowed. In Moab, the people worshiped Chemosh.

Chemosh, pagan god of prosperity, also called Molech—Scripture refers to him as an abomination to God—was a cast-iron, pot-bellied god who wore a pointed Phrygian cap—the same headgear of both Tammuz in Babylon, and later, Mithra in Rome. On

Winter Solstice, according to the ancient calendar,[4] a public child "mass" ["sacrifice"] was held. Pagan priests placed wood and pitch within iron image of the god Chemosh. When it became a red-hot furnace, the people made lists of their wishes for the coming year and recited their wishes to Chemosh, the god of prosperity. They then put their infants into the red-hot lap of the metal Chemosh to be incinerated, their religion assuring them their sacrifice would be rewarded in the upcoming year. The date? December 25th.

December 25th was also the day Egyptians worshipped their sun god, Ra. An Egyptian hieroglyph depicts the Egyptian sun god castrating himself—the same action Greek mythology attributes to Attis. Ra's worshippers would then hang gold and silver balls on an upright palm tree, placing their decorated offerings to the sun god under the tree adorned with the gold and silver testicles of Ra.

> Hear the word which the Lord says to you, O house of Israel. Thus says the Lord: 'Do not learn the way of the Gentiles; do not be dismayed at the signs of heaven, for the Gentiles are dismayed at them. For the customs of the peoples are futile; for one cuts a tree from the forest, the work of the hands of the workman, with the ax. They decorate it with silver and gold; they fasten it with nails and hammers so that it will not topple. (Jeremiah 10:1-4)

Israel adopted the custom of celebrating Ra's birthday on December 25th. They, too, used a green tree they had cut with an axe and erected in their homes so it wouldn't topple, decorating it with gold and silver balls. Because of the origin, God the Almighty calls this festival 'an abomination.'

> But the Lord is the true God; He is the living God and the everlasting King. At His wrath the earth will tremble, and the nations will not be able to endure His indignation. (Jeremiah 10:10)

In the 1600's, it was illegal in America to have a Christmas service or even a Christmas tree. The pilgrims knew that it as pure pagan sun god worship. In fact, Christmas was all but dying out in England when Charles Dickens revived it by writing his now famous *"Twas the Night Before Christmas."*

The reason we celebrate Easter is just as bad. Again, according to myth, when Tammuz the sun god was 40 years old, he was gored to death by a wild boar. Tammuz' lover (some versions say his mother) searched for him. She found him but he was minus his reproductive organ. For forty days she searches while earth women mourn. (See God's chastisement of the Jewish women for participating in this.[5]) Finally, on the fortieth day, he is restored and together they reappear on earth, amidst much hilarity and feasting. It was Constantine the Great, supposed benefactor of the church, who changed the date of the Old Testament feast of Passover to coincide with this ungodly festival.[6]

Sound familiar? The myth just keeps enlarging. When Nimrod's wife, Semiramas, who is Tammuz' mother, died as the exalted *Mother of God/Queen of Heaven,* she was sent back to earth in a giant egg which landed in the Euphrates River. Breaking open, she emerged as the reincarnated bare breasted goddess of fertility and sexual desire. With the new name, Ishtar (highly reminiscent of 'Easter),' she proves her divinity by changing a bird into an egg-laying rabbit![7]

There are ugly traditions associated with Easter/Ishtar. There are Canaanite caves in the Hinnom Valley in Jerusalem where caves were designated for the worship of Easter and her son Tammuz. There the priests of Easter would impregnate virgins as worship to Ishtar at the sunrise service. One year later the priests would sacrifice those three-month old infants on the same altar to Ishtar. This was the child sacrifice that was so notoriously connected with the original pagan ceremonies connected with the worship of the fertility goddess Ishtar. Easter egg origins is similarly ugly.[8]

Easter Sunday (often called 'Resurrection Day' by today's Christian church) is the day that concluded the 40 days of weeping for Tammuz' lost penis—how shamefaced we should be as we celebrate Lent and Easter, now that we know its true origins. From the time of its inception in Nimrod's Babylon until today, "this 40 day pagan festival climaxes as the sun god worshipers kill "the wild boar that killed

Tammuz" and eat "ham" after the Easter sunrise orgy and child sacrifice service."[9]

That is one day you can be assured that Y'shua of Nazareth did not rise from the grave—nor did He ever participate in the rehearsal of child sacrifice and fertility rites of pagan sun god worshippers.

Author Rood asks, "Now do you understand why the Holy One instructed us, "Do not learn the way of the heathen and how they worship their gods, and then do the same to Me."[10]

---

[1] *The Pagan-Christian Connection Exposed* by Michael J. Rood.
[2] Ibid. 85.
[3] Ibid.
[4] www.thechurchesofgod.com/CHRISTMAS.htm
[5] Ezekiel 8:14
[6] En.wikipedia.org/wiki/Quartododecimanism
[7] www.bibletruth.cc/Body_Easter.htm
[8] www.goodnewsaboutgod.com/studies/spiritual/home_study/gehenna.htm
[9] Hislop, 102-104, www.hope-of-israel.org/lent.htm
[10] Deuteronomy 12:30, 31

17
THE MISSING PUZZLE PIECE

It bears repeating. The God of the Bible has a Son and, at first glance one could be tempted to lump Him together with the other religions. After all, He does have a mother.

However, only the God of the Bible allowed His Son to be killed for the misdeeds of others. Only the God of the Bible opens wide the doors of heaven for those who repent of their misdeeds and ask to be covered by the sacrifice of His Son.

And, in biblical Christianity, the mother is just the mother. She does not claim for herself any manner of divineness. She is no goddess! Still, for those searching for the truth, we are left with the twin questions of which religions came first and which is the true religion.

The whole world is covered with goddess-claiming religions. Just look around. Hinduism is one, the Mormons believe they will become gods and goddesses, Buddha, Zoraster, Baal are glorified as spiritual beings. How did all this happen? Why are there spiritual beings—besides Jesus and God the Father—that are worshiped across the world if they are not the true God and true religions?

It all goes back to the Garden of Eden. God never tried to hide His plan for redeeming humanity from their sins. Indeed, at the same time that He was explaining the consequences of the first sins, He also provided us with hope because a Savior who was coming who would remove those sins. Speaking to the serpent who had led the man and woman into sin, God said:

> I will put enmity between you and the woman, and between your seed and her Seed; He shall bruise your head, and you shall bruise His heel. (Genesis 3:15)

This Seed who was to be the final sacrifice for sin had already been chosen—it was to be Jesus, God's own Son. Not only that, but *knowledge of that fact* was known before the foundation of the world!

> [Jesus] was chosen before the creation of the world, but was revealed in these last times..." I Peter 1:20 (NIV)

Even more than His having been chosen before the creation of the world, however, was the fact that the Bible tells us He was *sacrificed* at or before the time of creation. Thus His full title as revealed in the Revelation is *"the Lamb slain from the foundation of the world."* (Revelation 3:18)

What could this mean? So, is this time warp? Is this *an allusion* to time warp? We don't know. Maybe; maybe not. What we do know is that the sacrifice of Jesus – the Lamb of God that takes away the sin of the world – was a "done deal" before the creation of the world. (I John 1:29)

From Creation to the time of Jesus' death, all that remained was for His identity to be revealed. Well, that's not quite true—all that awaited was for His identity to be revealed *and His resurrection.*

The enemy of our souls, Satan, as well as all the angelic host, were witnesses to the fact from the beginning. God's Son was to be sacrificed and there would be a world full of sin. He had heard God speak prophetically that there would be a Seed born of a woman that would "bruise his head." He was, after all, the serpent in the Garden who heard the words straight from God's mouth.

He knew the word was true, but he did not repent. Instead, he devised a plan to slay the Seed himself. He seemed to have believed that if he killed the Seed, rather than God Himself being able to present the Seed in a proper sacrificial manner *on that day*, then he (Satan) would get the upper hand – and win. Not so.

Satan, the enemy of God and of our souls, made a fatal mistake. He did not know the deeper mysteries, the most secret parts of God's plan hidden even from Moses and the Old Testament heroes.

> "The secret things belong to the LORD our God, but those things which are revealed belong to us and to our children forever, that we may do all the words of this law." Deuteronomy 29:29.

Contrast the above declaration of secrecy with the

post-resurrection declaration that "the mystery kept secret" had finally been revealed:

> "Now to Him who is able to establish you according to …the revelation of the mystery kept secret since the world began *but now made manifest*…" Romans 16:25-26 (emphasis mine).

God chose not to allow the fullness of His plan to be divulged to the spiritual world. He did not give Satan *that additional piece* of information—the Resurrection!

> . . . the wisdom of God in a mystery, the hidden wisdom which God ordained before the ages for our glory, which none of the rulers of this age knew; for had they known, they would not have crucified the Lord of glory [Jesus]. (I Corinthians 2:7-8)

The Bible says Satan would never have killed the Seed (Jesus, the Son of God) had he known.

18
TWO TREES

In the center of the Garden of Eden, there were two trees. One was the Tree of Life; one was the Tree of the Knowledge of Good and Evil. The Tree of Life was meant to be eaten; the Tree of the Knowledge of Good and Evil, although attractive in appearance, was forbidden because it caused spiritual death.

Thus, just as there were dueling Mysteries in the universe, there were also opposing Trees—one holy and born of our Creator; the other conceived by His enemy. The thing about trees is that, though they are designed to bear fruit only after their own kind, they can be cross-pollinated.

In this way, hybrids can be formed, intentionally or unintentionally. When referring to natural trees, such cross-pollination can bring forth strains that are more (or less) resistant to diseases and pests; are hardier (or less hardy), and which visibly resemble one parent species more than the other.

The same is true of religions that combine, forming a syncretism; both will be changed into something new, and a different religion will emerge. In the Garden of Eden, Adam and Eve were told to eat from any of the trees except the Tree of the Knowledge of Good and Evil. This included the Tree of Life.

They were told that disobedience consisted of eating fruit from the forbidden tree. Period. It did not matter whether they ate from any other tree; to be obedient meant they had not eaten from the Tree of the Knowledge of Good and Evil. It was, as it were, a commandment. Spiritually speaking, there was *no* in-between, or hybrid, tree. It was black and white—a good tree bears good fruit; a bad tree bears bad fruit.[cxlii]

The clearest example of this is the nation of Israel at the time of the prophets. The nation as a whole, led by its priests and false prophets, was participating in Temple worship so it never abandoned the worship of the one True God; but these were not Israel's only worship services. They were also participating in the goddess religions of the neighboring nations. Pagan rites were being introduced into the Temple itself.

That may have angered God even more than if they had not worshiped Him at all, for God knew they knew the true way.[cxliii] The syncretism they were involved in served to give the Israelites a false sense of security but the demeaning practice did not appease or fool God.

Because of their idolatry which God repeatedly refers to as "harlotry," He forcibly removed them from the Promised Land and scattered them among the nations. There they remained until 1948, when God restored the Land to them just as He promised their ancestors centuries before. The important part of this story to remember, however, is that the Israelites' lukewarm worship of the God of the Bible, their Creator, *did not save them.* Likewise, when it comes to spiritual matters—it's our choice—**but *there is no acceptable hybrid.***

Using the Two-Tree test, take a look around at the contemporary churches that still teach an infant baptism even though it has its roots in paganism. The Bible says that you will know the tree by its fruit. Any branch of the Church that is rooted in the purity of biblical teachings will produce and re-produce the holy fruit that a holy God requires. Thus, you will recognize the *True Church*.

On the other hand, any branch that calls itself "church" but holds pagan views and does not follow the pattern set out for the Church in the Book of Acts is hybrid in character. It is not the True Church.

It is better to know ahead of time if you have been sitting in church pews but accepting a syncretism—a mishmash of religions patched together—but not the God of the Bible. Some will see a clear division between doctrines and actions that define the True Church and those that characterize the false church—and they will run toward truth. They will search for reconciliation with God as hard and as furiously as Luther did.[cxliv]

Others will, for the first time, recognize the difference between their church's beliefs and biblical Christianity but choose not to humble themselves through repentance and baptism so that they might close the chasm between themselves and God.

So, yes, this book will be polarizing, but it will get the job done. It isn't fair to be taught that everything is alright between you and God because you were baptized as an infant and then suddenly find out after death that you took a wrong turn.

It is for the enlightenment of those who attend infant baptism churches and desire to know if they were indeed saved when they were baptized as infants—that this book was written.

"What do we do then?" you ask, "Our children love Christmas with its beautiful lights and presents and Grandma and Grandpa and feasting and frosted cut-out cookies."

Well, Hanukkah is the *FESTIVAL OF LIGHTS*. Jesus Himself celebrated the Festival of Lights with His family. It occurs just a few days before Christmas and *lasts for eight days.* Plenty of time to visit friends and have them visit you. Plenty of time to give gifts and receive in return.

Plenty of time to celebrate Jesus Christ in beautiful and sacred ceremonies.

Ask your pastor and perhaps your church can begin celebrating the Festival of Lights and Jesus' *real* birthdate as a congregation!

The End

CHAPTER 18 ENDNOTE

1 Mathew 17:17-20
2 "So then, because you are lukewarm, and neither cold nor hot, I will vomit you out of My mouth."
Revelation 3:16
3 *The Question About Infant Baptism: Does Baptism Save?*

Appendix i

10 MYTHS OF INFANT BAPTISM

Myth 1: It is taught by some that babies are saved by infant baptism.

But the Bible does not say that. The following passage is almost always taken out of context. It is not about infant baptism. Jesus was responding to His disciples' question about which of them would be greatest in the kingdom of heaven.

> Then Jesus called a little child to Him, set him in the midst of them, and said, "Assuredly, I say to you, unless you are converted and become as little children, you will by no means enter the kingdom of heaven. Therefore whoever humbles himself as this little child is the greatest in the kingdom of heaven. —MATTHEW 18:2–4

Myth 2: It is taught by some that the following verse teaches a baptism of infants.

But the Bible does not say that. This verse is often taken out of context to refer to a baptism of infants even though there is no indication that Jesus sprinkled water on the children's heads. Jesus' method of laying-on of hands and praying was a typical Jewish blessing. Many denominations follow Jesus' example rather than infant baptism.

> Then little children were brought to Him that He might put His hands on them and pray, but the disciples rebuked them. But Jesus said, "Let the little children come to Me, and do not forbid them; for of such is the kingdom of heaven." And He laid His hands on them and departed from there.
> —MATTHEW 19:13–15

Myth 3: It is taught by some that infant baptism "saves" because Old Testament circumcision saved.

But the Bible says that Old Testament circumcision does not save. Nor did it ever. Therefore, if we are relying on the belief that infant baptism as a "thinly-veiled" *type* of circumcision "saves," we will fall from grace.

> Indeed I, Paul, say to you that if you become circumcised, Christ will profit you nothing....you who attempt to be justified by law [ritual]; you have fallen from grace...For in Christ Jesus neither circumcision nor uncircumcision avails anything, but faith working through love.
> —GALATIANS 5:2, 4, 6

> For we say that faith was accounted to Abraham for righteousness. How then was it

accounted? While he was circumcised, or uncircumcised? Not while circumcised, but while uncircumcised.

—ROMANS 4:9–10

Myth 4: It is taught by some that infant baptism is a type of Old Testament circumcision.

But the Bible does not say that. First, there is no record of infant baptisms in the New Testament church. Second, the Bible does not say that Infant Baptism is a thinly veiled type of circumcision (or any other kind).

Myth 5: It is taught by some that infant baptism is scriptural because all households included infants.

But the Bible does not say that. There are five examples of household baptisms given in the New Testament. In four examples, it is clear that all first believed and then were baptized.

> The jailer's household (See Acts 16:16–34, esp. v. 34.)
>
> Cornelius's household (See Acts 10:1–48, esp. vv. 1, 44.)
>
> Stephanas' household (See 1 Corinthians 16:15.)
>
> Crispus' household (See Acts 18:8.)

In the fifth example, the Bible does not specifically state that Lydia's whole household believed before they were baptized. On the other hand, it infers that this is true. We know Lydia and her household were devout believers in God. We know that the apostle Paul expounded the gospel to all gathered at the river for their prayer time and that all responded to his preaching by being baptized, so they probably were believers. But, the Bible is silent on that point. Thus, infant baptism theology seems to rest on the silence of this verse, since the Bible clearly states that circumcision does not save and, in fact, causes one to fall from grace.

Myth 6: It is taught by some that infant baptism is necessary so that babies do not go into *Limbo* should they die prematurely.

But the Bible does not say that. It says that God considers the offspring of believers to be holy. This is the same word *holy*, as used in the Bible for the Holy Spirit. God would not send His Holy Spirit to hell, and believer's babies do not go into hell (Limbo).

> For the unbelieving husband is sanctified by the wife, and the unbelieving wife is sanctified by the husband; otherwise your children would be *unclean*, but now they are *holy*.
> —1 CORINTHIANS 7:14, EMPHASIS ADDED

The infant baptism myth about babies dying and going into Limbo does not come from the Bible. It comes out of the mythology of heathenism. The reader of Greek and Roman classics will recognize Limbo from the Roman drama *The Aeneid*. Written by the well-known author Virgil, it tells of the plight of his character *Aeneas*.

The story tells of Aeneas's visit to the horrific

sulfur and flame-filled regions of the netherworld. There Aeneas finds the souls of tormented babies who, having been torn from their mother's breasts in death, must remain in Limbo outside hell's gates without ever having hope of heaven because their parents had not made sure they were given the rites of baptism before they died.

> Before the gates the cries of babes newborn, whom fate had from their tender mothers torn, assault his ears.[1]

Virgil's character in the play speaks of wretched babes who fate has forever sentenced to spend their eternity next to foolish persons who prematurely threw their life away through suicide. Many false ideas were added to Church doctrines by those who had previously been steeped in Greek mythology and the goddess and mystery religions.

> The next in place and punishment are they who prodigally threw their souls away, fools, who, repining at their wretched state, and loathing anxious life, suborned their fate.[2]

In other words, out of ancient Roman mythology comes the belief that a baptism of babies is necessary so they don't die and go to hell (go into Limbo). For centuries, the Roman Catholic Church taught a belief in something called Limbo, but on December 5, 2006, the pope called a news conference to let the world know that they had changed their mind. Babies would not now be sent to Limbo if they died unbaptized.

Pope Benedict XVI said that, all along, Limbo had merely been a hypothesis of their church. Because they were getting so many calls from distraught grandparents and mothers about what happened to aborted babies, he said they decided to drop Limbo from Catholic beliefs.

Myth 7: It is taught by some theologians that infant baptism joins us to the family of God.

But the Bible doesn't say this. It says the Holy Spirit joins us to the family of God! Infant baptism is stealing credit for something done by God's Holy Spirit.

> For by one Spirit, we were all baptized into one body—whether Jews or Greeks, whether slaves or free—and have all been made to drink into one Spirit.
> —1 CORINTHIANS 12:13

Myth 8: It is taught by some that the Holy Spirit is given through infant baptism.

But the Bible does not say that. It says that the Holy Spirit is given by faith, in what Jesus did for us on the cross. The Bible says we cannot receive the Holy Spirit by a ritual, only by faith:

> O foolish Galatians!...Did you receive the Spirit by the works of the law, or by the hearing of faith? Are you so foolish? Having begun in the Spirit, are you now being made

perfect by the flesh?…For as many as are of the works of the law are under the curse; for it is written, "Cursed is everyone who does not continue in all things which are written in the book of the law, to do them." But that no one is justified by the law in the sight of God is evident, for "the just shall live by faith." —GALATIANS 3:1–3, 10–11

Myth 9: It is taught by some that because John the Baptist sovereignly received the Holy Spirit while still in his mother's womb, that the Holy Spirit can be imparted by a minister during infant baptism.

But this is not true today. John the Baptist was of a different dispensation. During the Old Testament times, the Holy Spirit anointed for service (sovereignly came upon) prophets, kings, and priests for a specific task. John the Baptist's situation was that he was anointed to be a prophet while still in his mother's womb, and thus the Spirit of God was given to him at that time. The old covenant was in effect at that time because Jesus had not yet shed His Blood, which ratified the new covenant. But under the new covenant, there are no examples given of the Holy Spirit empowering people before they are born.

Myth 10: It is taught by some that the Great Commission teaches that baptism saves.

The Bible does not teach this. It specifically states that salvation is by faith, for it says that if one does not believe, he will be condemned.

> He who believes and is baptized will be saved; but he who does not believe will be condemned. —MARK 16:16

It is important to note the word *saved* in this passage does not only mean "going to heaven." It also means deliverance and provision while here on earth.

> The word "saved" is used indiscriminately by evangelical Christians while meaning "justified." Western Christianity uses the term "saved" when they talk about that moment in time when they receive a converted heart but this is inaccurate because the Bible uses the term "justified" in referring to that moment. It reserves the term "saved" for the making-us-whole that occurs *after we are justified.* In other words, "saved" refers to what God does AFTER we are born again; i.e., the deliverance, healing and restoration that begins to take place in every area of our lives after our conversion. As a western Christian layperson writing to western Christians, the term "saved" will continue to be used in this book but do not get confused: "Saved" means being made whole AFTER our conversion experience. Justified—*just-as-if-I'd-never-sinned*—means the righteousness imparted to us when we first put our faith in the finished work of the cross. Thus when reading the Bible, it is important

to pay attention to whether "saved" or "justified" is used in a verse in order to extract the correct biblical meaning.

When the above verse is read with this knowledge in mind, the verse fits neatly into New Testament doctrine.

> Saved (Greek, *sozo*): *Save* means the spiritual and eternal salvation granted to new believers immediately upon their conversion. Included in the word, saved, is temporal deliverance, material provision, deliverance from danger, etc., as well as eternal life.[3]

Thus, a correct understanding of the Mark 16:16 verse which includes the word *saved*, would be as follows: "They who do not believe will be condemned; however, they who both believe and are baptized will receive future spiritual benefits because of their faith plus temporal benefits while down here on Earth when they become a Christian."

Appendix i Endnotes

[1] Virgil, *The Aeneid, Book 6.ll,* 576–578, Dryden's Translation—Original, ll, 427–429.
[2] Virgil, *The Aeneid, Book 6,* 586-589, Dryden's Translation—Original, ll, 434-436.
[3] *Hebrew-Greek Key Word Study Bible,* 1760.

Appendix ii

BACK TO FAITH ALONE

Jesus Christ, as our Redeemer, is coming soon. At that time, those who have placed their faith in Him but have not yet died and ascended to heaven will rise to meet Him in the air. In order to be accepted in this number, Jesus described an experience we must have. His terminology for it was "born again:"

> Jesus said: Verily, verily, I say unto thee, "Except a man be born again, he cannot see the kingdom of God…Marvel not that I said unto thee, Ye must be born again.
> (John 3:3, 7)

> Jesus said: I am the way, the truth, and the life. No one comes to the Father except through Me. (John 14:6)

> All that the Father gives Me will come to Me, and the one who comes to Me I will by no means cast out. (John 6:37)

> For all have sinned and fall short of the glory of God, being justified freely by His grace through the redemption that is in Christ Jesus, whom God set forth as a propi-

> tiation by His blood, though faith, to demonstrate His righteousness, because in His forbearance God had passed over the sins that were previously committed, to demonstrate at the present time His righteousness, that He might be just and the justifier of the one who has faith in Jesus.
> (Romans 3:23-26)

> If you confess with your mouth the Lord Jesus and believe in your heart that God has raised Him from the dead, you will be saved. For with the heart one believes unto righteousness, and with the mouth confession is made unto salvation ...Whoever believes on Him will not be put to shame ... For "whoever calls upon the name of the LORD shall be saved." (Romans 10:9-11-13)

God made it simple for us because He is not willing that any should perish.1 If you want eternal life and believe that Jesus is God's Son and that He died, was buried, and resurrected, tell Him. Pray your own prayer, or say something like this:

> *God, I believe that Jesus is Your only begotten Son and that He died, was buried, and that He rose again. I choose to make Jesus the Lord of my life. Come into my heart, Lord Jesus. Amen.*

Now, be baptized in water! Make Jesus truly Lord of your life. The Bible says, "Or do you not know that as many of us as were baptized into Christ Jesus were baptized in His death ... For IF we have been united together in the likeness of His death, certainly we shall be *in the likeness of His* resurrection," (Rom.6:3-5).

> "Or do you not know that as many of us as were baptized into Christ Jesus were baptized into His death? Therefore we were buried with Him through baptism into death, that just as Christ was raised from the dead by the glory of the Father; even so we also should walk in newness of life. For if we have been united together in the likeness of His death, certainly we also shall be *in the likeness of His* resurrection,"(Romans 5:3-5)

In other words, water baptism is important. IF we die with Christ, we will also *rise to newness of life*. It is an action we take to show our faith in Christ's finished work of the cross on our behalf. Just as Abraham the Old Testament patriarch of our faith submitted to the ritual of circumcision to show his faith was genuine (at the same time, giving his descendants a ritual whereby they could also be included in God's covenant), we submit to water baptism—as a *type of spiritual circumcision*. (See Col.2:11-12.)

Being baptized into the name of Jesus Christ for the remission of sin is not an optional action. You are commanded to *"repent, be baptized into the name of Jesus Christ for the remission of sin,"* Acts 2:38,*"and you will receive the gift of the Holy Spirit."* While it does not save us (Christ's shed blood has already provided salvation) the Bible is quite clear that there is an "IF" included. IF we are united with Christ in water baptism, we will also rise to newness of life, (Rom.6:4).

What if we were baptized as infants? We are to be rebaptized! If we have been baptized into something other than Jesus' name, we are to be re-baptized. Rebaptism is not a problem for God. In the early Church, rebaptism was dealt with as a very unimportant issue as long as the new disciples received the Bible baptism of believers, that of the baptism into the name of Jesus. (See Acts 19:1-6.)

Then tell your priest or pastor that you want to take part in biblical water baptism. This means after conversion/full immersion baptism as done in the Book of Acts. The Bible says "let every one of you" take part in this baptism. It is for every believer. It is the way of the Cross.

God's provision for us was never to change until the second coming of Christ and includes receiving the gift of the Holy Spirit. In all the examples given in the Book of Acts after the Day of Pentecost, if the Holy Spirit was not openly manifested, before or after water baptism, disciples were dispatched to lay hands on them and bring them into that experience. Neither water baptism nor receiving the Holy Spirit was taken casually.[2]

If your pastor or priest won't baptize you (or rebaptize you) after you believe, God will help you find one that will, for this is the full program of God. Baptism doesn't save you, but it shows God that your faith is genuine.

> Repent, and let every one of you be baptized in the name of Jesus Christ for the remission of sins; and you shall receive the gift of the Holy Spirit. For the promise is to you and to your children, and to all who are afar off, as many as the Lord our God will call.
> (Acts 2:38-39)

Reflect and decide now. The Bible says that faith without actions is dead.[3] Jesus commanded baptism.[4] Be baptized in water *and in the Spirit*...

Appendix ii Endnotes

[1] 2 Peter 3:9

[2] Samaritans—Acts 8:1, 17; Ethiopian eunuch—Acts 8:26–38; Saul/Paul's conversion—Acts 9:1–19; Cornelius's household—Acts 10:1–48; Lydia's household—Acts 16:11–15; Philippians jailer's household—Acts 16:25–34; the Ephesians—Acts 19:1–10

[3] James 2:17

[4] Matthew 28:19; Mark 16:16

AUTHOR'S PAGE

As a layperson, Judith McClary has had a deep interest in Christian spirituality and theology all of her adult life. It has been her joy to study Scripture in formal and informal Christian settings and in daily personal life. Curiosity over why the Church has two different branches, two different water baptisms and two wildly-different teachings about salvation—one teaching that baptism 'saves' and the other teaching it does not—has led her to her Bible for the truth about infant baptism. McClary has been a pre-school department supervisor, elementary-age Sunday school coordinator, teacher of both teens and adults, board member of *Presbyterian Renewal*, T-V assistant, film editor, and camera person for *The Pastor's Study,* a leader of spiritual growth groups with her husband, writer of Bible curriculum, hospital care minister and she has authored several books. Currently she and her husband are prayer team members at a six-location, community church that had over 44,000 visitors and members during the 2014 Christmas weekend. To contact the author or invite her to speak; e-mail or visit her website:

judymcclary@gmail.com
www.doesbaptismsave.com

BOOKS BY THE AUTHOR

WILL THE REAL CHURCH PLEASE STAND UP series

1 THE SECRET ABOUT INFANT BAPTISM THAT EVERYONE'S MISSING – Asked by her church to write a 12-week Bible course, the author uncovers the origins of infant baptism and Luther's flip-flop. Must reading for those who think their baptism saved them.

2 A SINKING SHIP: THE INFANT BAPTISM SAGA – A look at St. Malachy's prophecy and Pope Francis' Jesuit background. A historical look at the deadly duo of Roman Catholicism and the early founders of Protestantism as they kill Christian and Jew over infant baptism.

3 HOMOSEXUALITY IN THE CHURCH: A SECOND LOOK AT THE RE-IMAGINING CONFERENCES – Are the goddess religions shadowing the churches that sponsored the RE-imagining conferences? Homosexuals in the pulpit and worship of a pagan goddess are traced back to the "RE-imagining" conferences during the decade of the '90s.

4 SEVEN LETTERS TO THE INFANT BAPTISM CHURCH: *A Layperson Speaks Out* – Seven letters to her Lutheran church as, step-by-step, the author researches Church history and uncovers the origins of infant baptism.

5 WATER BAPTISM: *GOD'S TEST* – God gave the Jews a way to prove their faith was genuine under the old covenant. What about us? Read about God's test for the new covenant believer.

6 I WENT TO BAPTIST KID'S CAMP & CAME HOME SPEAKING IN TONGUES : *A Holy Ghost Story* - An unchurched child receives the Book of Acts experience when she attends Bible camp with a friend. Read how her born-again experience with evidence of tongues changed her life forever.

7 A DARK HORSE? MORMON CHURCH & THE ANTICHRIST - A forgotten Mormon massacre and excerpts from a book written in 1834 just 12-years after Joseph Smith, Jr. started his Mormon religion reveals the origins of the manuscript he immortalized as the '*Book of Mormon*.'

BIBLIOGRAPHY

Alex, Ben. *Martin Luther: The German Monk Who Changed the Church.* Victor Books/SP Publications, Inc., 1995.

Anderson, Sir Norman. *Christianity and World Religions.* Leicester, England: InterVarsity Press, 1984.

Arendzen, J. P. "Gnosticism," *New Advent: The Catholic Encyclopedia,* Vol. 6. New York, 1909. www.newadvent.org.

Armstrong, O. K. and Armstrong M. M. *The Indomitable Baptists.* Garden City, NJ: Doubleday & Company, 1967.

Beale, J. L. *Rise to Newness of Life.* Nappanee, IN: Evangel Press, 1974.

Bettenson, H. S., ed. *Documents of the Christian Church,* 2nd ed. London, England: Oxford University Press, 1963.

Bingham, D. Jeffrey. *Pocket History of the Church.* Downers Grove, IL: InterVarsity Press, 2002.

Booker, R. *The Miracle of the Scarlet Thread.* Shippensburg, PA: Destiny Image Publishers, 1981.

Brant, I. *James Madison: 1787-1800.* Indianapolis, IN: Bobbs-Merrill Company, 1950.

Broadbent, E. H. *The Pilgrim Church.* Grand Rapids, MI: Gospel Folio Press, 1999.

Brim, B. *The Blood and the Glory.* Tulsa, OK: Harrison House, 1995.

Bruce, F. F. *The International Bible Commentary with the NIV.* Grand Rapids, MI: Zondervan Publishing House, 1979.

Bruce. F. F. *The Spreading Flame.* Grand Rapids, MN: Wm. B. Erdmans Publishing, 1995.

The Catechism of the Catholic Church. Mahwah, NJ: Paulist Press, 1994.

Dake, Finis Jennings. *Dake's Annotated Reference Bible.* Lawrencevill, GA. Dake Publishing, Inc. 1999.

Davies, J. G. *The Early Christian Church.* New York: Holt, Rinehart, and Winston, 1965.

DeArteaga, W. *Quenching the Spirit: Examining Centuries of Opposition to the Movement of the Holy Spirit.* Lake Mary, FL: Creation House, 1992.

Dickens, A. G. *The Counter Reformation.* New York: Harcourt, Brace & World, 1969.

Dolan, J. P. *History of the Reformation.* New York: Descleo Company, 1965.

Dyck, C. J., ed. *An Introduction to Mennonite History.* Scottsdale, PA: Herald Press, 1967.

Erikson, E. H. *Young Man Luther: A Study in Psychoanalysis and History.* New York, NY: Norton, 1958.

Foxe, J. *Foxe's Books of Martyrs.* Springdale, PA: Whitaker House, 1981.

Foxe, John, rewritten and updated by Harold J. Chadwick, *Foxe's Book of Martyrs: Updated to the 21st Century.* Gainesville, FL: Bridge-Logos, 2001.

Friedenthal, R. *Luther: His Life and Times.* New York: Harcourt, Brace & Jovanovich, 1970.

Gollian, G. L. *Moravian in Two Worlds.* New York: Columbia University Press, 1967.

Grimm, H. J. *The Reformation Era: 1500-1650.* New York: Macmillan, 1973.

Gundry, R. H. *A Survey of the New Testament,* 3rd ed. Grand Rapids, MI: Zondervan Publishing House, 1994.

Hayford, J. *Hayford's Bible Handbook.* Nashville, TN: Thomas Nelson Publishers, 1995.

Hinn, B. *The Blood.* Orlando, FL: Creation House, 1993.

Hislop, A. *The Two Babylons.* Neptune, NJ: Loizeaux Brothers, 1916.

Horn, W. M. *Growth in Grace.* Philadelphia, PA: Muhlenberg Press, 1951.

Hostetler, J. A. *Hutterite Society*. Baltimore, MD: John Hopkins University Press. 1974.

Hostetler, J. & Huntington, G. *The Hutterites in North America.* New York: Holt, Rinehart, and Winston, 1980.

Huggins, L. *The Blood Speaks.* South Plainfield, NJ: Bridge Publications, 1954.

Hunt, D. *A Woman Rides the Beast.* Eugene, OR: Harvest House Publishers, 1994.

Hurstfield, J. *The Reformation Crisis*. New York: Barnes & Noble, 1965.

Inter-Lutheran Commission on Worship. *The Lutheran Book of Worship.* Minneapolis, MN: Augsburg Publishing House, 1978.

Jensen, I. L. *Jensen's Survey of the Old Testament.* Chicago, IL: Moody Press, 1978.

Kempis, T. *The Imitation of Christ.* London: Oxford University Press, 1920.

Kenyon, E. W. *The Blood Covenant, 28th ed.* Lynnwood, WA: Kenyon's Gospel Publishing Society, 1969.

KJV-Amplified Holy Bible: Parallel Bible. Grand Rapids, MI: Zondervan Publishing House, 1995.

Leonard, E. G., Reid, J. M., trans. and ed. Rowley, H. H. *A History of Protestantism: The Reformation,. Vol. 1.* Indianapolis, IN: Bobbs-Merrill, 1968.

Loewen, Harry and Nolt, Steven. *Through Fire & Water: An Overview of Mennonite History*. Scottsdale, PA: Herald Press, 1996.

Lohse, M. *Martin Luther: An Introduction to His Life and Work*. Philadelphia, PA: Fortress Press, 1986.

Luther, M. *Ninety-Five Theses: Address to the German Nobility Concerning Christian Liberty.* New York: Collier, 1965.

Manns, P. *Martin Luther: An Illustrated Biography*. New York: Crossroad, 1982.

McClary, J. M. *The Secret About Infant Baptism That Everyone's Missing*. (Lake Mary, FL. Creation House. 2008.)

Mjorud, H. *What's Baptism All About?* Carol Stream, IL: Creation House, 1978.

Murray, A. *The Power of the Blood of Jesus.* Springdale, PA: Whitaker House, 1993.Norris, R. A., Jr. *The Christological Controversy.* Philadelphia, PA: Fortress Press, 1980.

Oberman, H. *Luther: A Man Between God and the Devil.* New Haven, CT: Yale University Press, 1989.

O'Donnell, J. J. *Augustine.* Boston, MA: Twayne Publishers, 1985.

Office of the Presbyterian General Assembly. *The Work of the Holy Spirit.* Philadelphia, PA: United Presbyterian Church in the United States of America, 1978.

O'Neill, J. *Martin Luther.* New York: Cambridge University Press, 1975.

Oyer, J. S. and Kreider, R. S. *Mirror of the Martyrs.* Intercourse, PA: Good Books, 1990.

Prince, D. *Appointment in Jerusalem.* Grand Rapids, MI: Chosen Books, 1975.

Reimer, M. L., ed. *Christians Courageous.* Waterloo, Ontario: Mennonite Publishing Service, 1988.

Richardson, D. *Eternity in Their Hearts.* Ventura, CA: Regal Books, 1981.

Rives, Richard M. *Too Long in the Sun.* (Partakers Publications, Charlotte, NC. 1997.

Rost, S., ed. *Martin Luther: The Best From All His Works.* Nashville, TN: Thomas Nelson, 1989.

Sachar, Leon, Ph.D. *A History of the Jew, 5th ed.* New York: Alfred A. Knopf, 1967.

Simon, E. *Luther Alive: Martin Luther and the Making of the Reformation.* Garden City, NY: Doubleday, 1968.

Schmeman, Alexander. *The Historical Road of Eastern Orthodoxy.*

Smith, C. H. *Story of the Mennonites.* Newton, KS: Mennonite Publication Office, 1950.

Spitz, L. W. *The Protestant Reformation.* Englewood Cliffs, NJ: Prentice-Hall, 1966.

Strong, J. *The Strong's Exhaustive Concordance of the Bible.* Nashville, TN: Thomas Nelson Publishers, 1996.

Tenney, M. C. *New Testament Times.* Grand Rapids, MN: Wm B. Erdmans Publishing Company, 1978.

Todd, J. M. *Luther.* New York: Crossroad, 1982.

Trumbull, H. C. *The Blood Covenant: A Primitive Rite and Its Bearing on Scripture.* Kirkwood, MO: Impact Books, 1975.

van Braght, T. J. *Martyrs Mirror.* Scottsdale, PA: Herald Press, 1950.

Vine, W.E. *Vine's Expository Dictionary of Old & New Testament Words.* Nashville, TN. Thomas Nelson, Inc., 1997.

The Waldenses. Angwin, CA: LLT Productions.

White, Ellen G. *The Great Controversy.* Mt. View, CA: Pacific Press Publ. Assn., 1956.

Whyte, Rev. H. A. M. *The Power of the Blood.* Springdale, PA: Whitaker House, 1973.

"Worshipping Like Pagans?" *Christian History*, Issue 37.

Yandian, B. *Galatians: The Spirit-Controlled Life.* Tulsa, OK: Pillar Book & Publishing Company, 1993.

www.ingramcontent.com/pod-product-compliance
Lightning Source LLC
Chambersburg PA
CBHW060156050426
42446CB00013B/2861